CONQUEST OF MIND

★

ALSO BY EKNATH EASWARAN

★

Gandhi the Man

The Bhagavad Gita for Daily Living

Meditation

Dialogue with Death

A Man to Match His Mountains

The Compassionate Universe

Thousand Names of Vishnu

God Makes the Rivers to Flow

Words to Live By

Your Life Is Your Message

Climbing the Blue Mountain

The Unstruck Bell

Take Your Time

The Undiscovered Country

★

FOR CHILDREN

The Monkey & the Mango

★

CLASSICS OF INDIAN SPIRITUALITY

The Bhagavad Gita

The Dhammapada

The Upanishads

★

CLASSICS OF CHRISTIAN INSPIRATION

Love Never Faileth

Original Goodness

Seeing with the Eyes of Love

CONQUEST OF MIND

EKNATH EASWARAN

NILGIRI PRESS

ISBN: cloth, 0–915132–51–6; paper, 0–915132–50–8

Third Printing March 1997

The Blue Mountain Center of Meditation, founded in Berkeley,
California, in 1961 by Eknath Easwaran, publishes books on how to
lead the spiritual life in the home and the community. For information
please write to Nilgiri Press, Box 256, Tomales, California 94971

Library of Congress Cataloging-in-Publication Data

Easwaran, Eknath.
      Conquest of mind / by Eknath Easwaran.
        p.   cm.
      ISBN 0–915132–51–6
      ISBN 0–915132–50–8 (pbk.)
        1. Meditation.   2. Spiritual life.   I. Title.
BL627.E168 1988
158'. 12 – dc19   88–26575
                                    CIP

Table of Contents

Introduction

"ALL THAT WE ARE," the Buddha said, "is the result of what we have thought." He might have added, "And all we shall become is the result of what we think now."

Nothing, then, can be more important than being able to choose the way we think — our feelings, aspirations, and desires; the way we view our world and ourselves. Mastery of the mind opens avenues of hope. It means that we can begin to reshape our life and character, rebuild relationships, thrive in the stress of daily living, become the kind of person we want ourselves to be.

In this book I present the art of training the mind how to respond to life's challenges, drawing on almost thirty years of teaching meditation to an American audience. Each chapter was originally a talk given to a select group of students. I touch on theory, but the emphasis is always practical and down to earth. I have written for those who want to understand not only how the mind works, but also how it can be changed — which means, in this context, those who are interested in the actual practice of meditation.

Today we hear "meditation" used to describe a number of things, some of which have nothing to do with meditation as I understand it. These techniques may be relaxing, they may be inspiring, they may be good for your physical health, but as far as accomplishing enduring, beneficial changes in the mind, they have no more effect than writing on water. There are also time-honored methods of meditation which differ from the one I teach: for example, watching the flow of thoughts in detachment, without any attempt at control. I respect these methods in the hands of an illumined teacher, but confusion can result from mixing instructions that come from different perspectives. If you want to become a tennis champion, you don't take lessons from Vic Braden and Nick Bollettieri at the same time; they have utterly different approaches to the game. Meditation teachers have different approaches too, and it is good to remember that two people who say they meditate may be doing very dissimilar things.

When I talk about meditation, I am referring to a dynamic discipline that would be recognized in any of the major spiritual traditions of the world: teaching attention to flow without a break toward a single inspirational focus within the mind (in this case, the memorized words of an inspirational passage) until finally the mind becomes completely absorbed and all distracting thoughts disappear. In this profound absorption the mind is still, calm, and clear. This is our native state. Once we become established in it, we know once and for all who we are and what life is for. As the Bible puts it, "Be still, and know that I am God."

In these pages I will often refer to the "great mystics" of the world. This word "mystic," too, is easily misunderstood. Mysticism is the conviction, born of personal experience, that there is a divine core in human personality which each of us can realize directly, and that making this discovery is the real goal of our lives. A mystic is anyone who has achieved this goal. The great mystics speak the same language, for they come from the same country of the soul. Their ranks include such luminous figures as Saint Francis of Assisi, Saint Teresa of Avila, Sri Ramakrishna, the Compassionate Buddha, and Mahatma Gandhi, among many others equally well known and relatively unknown.

Whenever I describe the mechanics of meditation in this book, I will always be referring to the method I teach, which I have practiced myself for many decades. It is essentially the training of attention. The technique is simple but far from easy. It requires effort, and — like athletic conditioning — it can be quite strenuous. Its purpose is not to attain some remarkable experience during meditation but to master the thinking process. The rewards, therefore, come during the rest of the day. As your meditation deepens, you will find yourself stronger and more resilient, better able to face the challenges of life as the kind of person you would like to be: loving, creative, resourceful, and full of vitality.

At the end of this book I give a very brief summary of the eight-point program which I myself have followed. There you will find instructions in meditation along with an introduction to seven very helpful practices, such as slowing down, which extend the benefits of meditation into daily living. (This program is elaborated in detail in my book *Meditation,* which has a full chapter on each point.) If you are not already familiar with these points from my other books, you might want to look now at the summary beginning on page 175 in order to get the most from the chapters that follow.

PART I

Thinking in Freedom

Thinking in Freedom

NOT LONG AGO my wife and I went for an early morning walk on a secluded beach near our home. The coastline in northern California can be rugged, and on this stretch the waves were uncommonly high. I found myself absorbed in watching a huge log with which the sea was playing like a cat. Wave after wave carried the log onto the shore and then rolled it back, unresisting, in the curl of the backwash. Finally a huge swell swept it far up onto the sand. It lay there sodden, as if to say, "I came here all by myself, and now I'm going to stay here. I like this place." But a few minutes later another rush of water lifted it free again and carried it back into the sea. Along it went without a sign of protest, buffeted and rolled at the pleasure of the waves.

I couldn't help feeling that for the most part, this is what our lives are like too. The Buddha would say that most of us live at the mercy of circumstances, going wherever life takes us. Even those whom the world calls great, especially if we look beyond their sphere of greatness, often seem to have had scant say in their lives: they may have conquered many thousands, for example, yet lived at the mercy of their own whims and passions. Like the Buddha, we might observe these vagaries and wonder to ourselves, "Is that all there is to life, being buffeted to and fro by circumstances until the show is over? Is that the best a human being can manage?"

As a former professor of English literature, when I saw those massive waves bearing down with the foam on their crests tossed by the wind, I immediately recalled some lines from Byron describing the "white manes of the sea." I felt as if horses were charging down on me, and my first impulse was, "The cavalry is coming. Let me run for my life!" It was a normal response. But far out in the water, I noticed with surprise, were two young fellows whose response was just the opposite. They had no desire for a glassy surface. They wanted waves, fierce waves, the bigger the better.

Coming from South India, I had never seen surfing until I came to California. The sport still fascinates me. I stood back and watched while one brave soul turned his back on a powerful swell and tried to get to his feet. The wave picked him up and tossed him aside into its crest, spinning his board into the air like a missile. If that had happened to me, I would have swum straight for the beach and hauled myself out on the sand, leaving my board to anyone who wanted to claim it. But this fellow was made of different stuff. He retrieved his board and waited there for the next wave to come. Again the same thing happened — and again he came back for more.

The other young man had more experience. He knew just where he wanted to be, and when the next wave rolled in he caught its pace with a couple of swift, sure strokes. In seconds he was on his feet, cutting back and forth along the face of that wall of water as if making the ocean do his bidding were the easiest thing in the world.

Suddenly the wave arched overhead and crashed down, apparently drowning the poor chap in an avalanche of water. I expected to see his board shoot into the air like his friend's. But a moment later, crouching like a runner ready to spring from the block, he shot triumphantly from a tunnel of spray and swung his board up over the back of the wave, out of danger. The same waves from which I had wanted to run, he had harnessed and learned to ride.

All of us, I think, would like to enjoy that kind of mastery in living. Who doesn't respond to the thought of taking life's waves and riding them with effortless grace? Countless books and tapes today appeal to our yearning for a key to life, or at least to a part of life, which only experts know: methods, secrets, tips, or tactics for mastering the forces that otherwise master us. To judge from the records of ancient civilizations, this must be one of the oldest of human desires. Is there a key to our destiny? If so, do we have a say in it, or are our character and fate fixed by the stars?

The Buddha's answer, set out more than twenty-five hundred years ago, has a very modern appeal. Our destiny, he said, lies in our own hands: "All that we are is the result of what we have thought. We are formed and molded by our thoughts." It follows that what we shall be tomorrow is shaped by what we think today. To this penetrating observation he added a simple twist. "Don't try to control the future," he would say. "Work on the one thing you *can* learn to control: your own responses."

If we merely react to life, this implies, we have no more freedom of choice than that log the ocean was playing with. We go where life pushes and pulls us. But if we can choose our responses, we have mastered life. Like a skilled surfer, we don't need to ask for perfect waves. Where is the challenge in that? We show our skill by how well we can handle whatever the sea sends.

"All that we are is the result of what we have thought." It sounds so simple, but this truth has far-reaching implications. The Buddha would go so far as to say that it is we who have made the circumstances we find ourselves in today. We have got ourselves into them by all the deep-seated ways of thinking that led us into the actions, plans, behavior, and situations whose sum total is our lives.

Yet this seems not quite fairly put, for not much of this has been done intentionally. We have exercised very little control over these thoughts. We say that we think our thoughts, but it would be more accurate to say that our thoughts think us.

How many times have you exclaimed, "I wish I could stop thinking that! I wish I could stop craving this. I wish I didn't always react like a vending machine to this kind of person or that kind of situation. I wish I could be different from the way I am!" The Buddha would reply, "You can." If you have felt this desire fervently, you have what it takes to learn to live in freedom.

This is not a book about the Buddha or his teachings, yet I will mention him often in these pages. The reason is simple: no one teaches more clearly that mastery of life depends on mastering the mind. If we want to grow to our fullest human stature, the Buddha would say, all we have to do is teach the mind how to think differently: how to be calm, kind, and creative in any situation.

In the modern world this is a very appealing approach, and for good reasons: it is rational, it is completely practical, and it puts our destiny in our own hands. And it is universal. Whether we are Christian or Jewish, Hindu or Buddhist, Muslim or atheist or agnostic, the human mind works the same way for all. Training the mind is the same for everyone.

Each of us would like to be able to think what he or she *wants* to think. Yet how many do you know who can do this? The mind is very much like a television set with no controls, which goes on when the mood strikes it and shows whatever it pleases.

Imagine that you are sitting in your living room, listening to little Joey tell you about his basketball game, when suddenly the television switches on. "Here," it commands. "Watch me!" You say, "Yes, sir." You don't like the program, and you don't really want to look at television when Joey is trying to talk to you. But the TV has caught your attention. The set says, "I feel like showing this now, so you sit back and watch." And while Joey goes on, you look at him occasionally and say, "Uh-huh," but you're not really there; your mind is on the tube.

Then, abruptly, the set announces, "That's it for now." And despite your pleas, it turns itself off.

Most of us, if we had a set like this, would think we

were caught in a science fiction movie. But this is exactly what the mind does. It puts on any show it likes and that is what we have to think; it switches channels when it likes and that is what we have to accept. "I can tell my hand what to do," Augustine once observed, "and it obeys. Why can't I do the same with my mind?"

Today, of course, most homes have a remote control device for the television set. You lean back in a chair, press a button, and the set goes on. If you don't like the commercial telling you what to have for breakfast, you press another button and the sound goes off. If you want to change channels, press a button; if you want to stop the show, just press again — whenever you choose. So when I go to a friend's home to watch tennis, my host puts the remote controller in my hands. I watch Boris Becker play Ivan Lendl, and the moment a commercial cuts in or the commentators start talking about how much money is at stake, I turn off the sound and rest my eyes. This is using television in freedom, and it is the way to use the mind in freedom too.

People sometimes object, "Having a trained mind sounds so mechanical! What about spontaneity, creativity?" Even with television, I think you will agree, nothing is more mechanical than sitting on the couch like a potato and watching whatever comes on. It is the same with the mind. Nothing is less spontaneous than thinking whatever pops into your head, because there you have no choice. Almost all thinking is conditioned, stimulus and response. Only when choosing in freedom does the human being truly come to life.

❧

What does it mean, then, to have the freedom to tell your mind what to think? I can give you one breathtaking example. All too often, personal relationships fall apart when the mind is untrained. The illustration with Joey gives a clue. When our attention can be captured by any little thing, we cannot show our children or partner much love; the mind will always be wandering off after something else. We move away from a marriage because our partner no longer interests us. We move away from friends because we get tired of their company. Some psychologists say we are becoming a nation of emotional drifters, moving from person to person as we move from place to place and from job to job.

The problem here is not really with other people. We do not lose interest in people because they get less interesting; we lose interest because our mind is restless. It is the nature of an untrained mind to keep moving, moving, moving. But the mind is infinitely teachable. You can make it natural for your mind not to move, but to dwell like a laser wherever you place it. That is the secret of genius, and it is the secret of satisfying relationships too. When you tell your mind "Stay," it will stay. You can keep giving Joey your full attention instead of letting it be snatched away by the TV. You can keep giving your partner your respect and love even if he gives you cause for feeling differently.

Most wonderfully, I think, you can bring back all the delight and freshness you first felt in any personal relationship. What made those moments memorable was that your attention was riveted on the object of your love. When your mind is trained, you can keep this sense of delight and wonder alive always; it will actually grow with the passage of time. This is the greatest wealth a human being can have: relationships that never turn stale or sour but go on growing in depth and beauty.

ã€‰

Yet how much dedication, how much hard work, are required to bring about these changes!

I remember the first time I saw Rudolf Nureyev, one of the greatest ballet stars of the modern world, doing scenes from *Swan Lake* and *Romeo and Juliet* — gliding and pirouetting without effort, springing into the air as gracefully as a deer. He has taught his body to listen to whatever his creative impulse commands, and to obey so effortlessly that defying gravity seems natural. You just run and leap, run and glide; it's not hard at all.

Later, in a documentary, I saw some of the scenes behind the scenes, where great dancers work at their art for five or six hours every day. Some of the exercises they were doing were most uninteresting — in fact, they were downright dull. We like to think of ballerinas as glamorous, doing glissades and leaps and pirouettes all day. The fact is that if you want to be a ballerina, you have to spend thousands of hours doing one of the most boring exercises I can imagine: clinging to a bar and kicking up your legs over and over, while you perspire and get more and more disheveled.

To me those dancers looked like galley slaves, standing there chained to the bars. The slave driver comes and says, "Now: *one,* two, three; *one,* two, three," and they kick, kick, kick, day in and day out. People like me would say, "I'm not interested, thank you. Where are the thrills? Where is the glamour? Who *is* that man to say 'one, two, three' and make me kick my heels in the air?" Yet this is what is required to train every part of the body to listen to you. Spontaneity, as any artist or athlete will confirm, comes only after lots and lots of disciplined practice.

That is exactly what I would say about training the mind. If a ballet star has to practice for hours every day, following a special routine under very watchful guidance, should we find it any easier to undo old, rigid, conditioned ways of thinking? The amazing thing is that it can be done at all — and that anybody can learn it, anybody who is prepared to put in the effort.

After seeing the kind of training Nureyev must have undergone, I realized anew why genius has been called just an infinite capacity for taking pains. Dancers like Nureyev *are* gifted, but their gift is not in having been born with the grace of a deer; it is their immense dedication. So too with the spiritual geniuses of the world: men and women like Teresa of Avila, the Compassionate Buddha, Francis of Assisi, Mahatma Gandhi. They also devoted their lives to training for mastery: not to be able to dance with ease but to be able to love with ease, to think in freedom, to make every response to life a matter of their free choice. By their lives they show us what it means to be a human being.

CHAPTER 2

Living Skills

WHEN I CAME TO BERKELEY as a Fulbright scholar in the early sixties, I found a house near a place called Live Oak Park. On the edge of the park sat a couple of tennis courts, and here several days a week the city had stationed a tennis coach with a very good reputation. I had played a bit of tennis in India and had enjoyed it, so I said to myself, "Why not go and benefit from his expertise?"

One morning I carried my racquet over and approached him. "All right," he said, "stand over there on the other side of the net and let's take a look at your game."

I ran to the other court. "Okay," he called, "go ahead and serve."

I tossed the ball in the air and hit it for all I was worth. He returned it nicely; I must say. We exchanged a few shots — you might even have called it a rally. I served a few more balls, and then he came to the net and looked at me. "Let's have a chat," he said.

I felt flattered. "In only five minutes," I asked myself, "have I impressed this coach so much? Maybe I have the makings of a Big Bill Tilden."

"Won't you sit down?" he said. Then he asked innocently, "Where did you learn to play like this?"

"Oh," I said, "in India. Right at my university."

"Who taught you?"

I had him there. "Nobody," I said. "I taught myself."

He grimaced. "That's what I thought!"

And like a really good coach, who is interested not so much in pleasing you as in improving your game, he started in without preamble: "The way you stand is wrong. The way you hold the racquet is wrong. The way you throw the ball in the air is wrong. The way you approach the ball and swing is wrong. Naturally," he added kindly, "the way you miss it is wrong too."

My face must have fallen, because he smiled and patted me on the shoulder. "There's no need to feel discouraged," he said. "That's how people who teach themselves tennis usually start." And he proceeded to give me a list of instructions, ticking them off on his fingers: one, two, three, four, five. "Start doing all this," he assured me, "and things will begin to go right."

My grandmother, my spiritual teacher, used this same approach to teach me how to live. You should not picture Granny as a gentle old lady in a rocking chair. She was active and vibrantly alive, tough and tender at the same time, and although she used words sparingly she made each one count. Clearly but compassionately, she would tell me just what I was doing wrong. Then, largely by her personal example, she would show me how to change.

Once, I remember, I got into a senseless squabble with a classmate and came home hurt and angry. Granny took one look at my red eyes and asked, "What happened, son?"

With the simplicity of youth I replied, "Raman called me names."

My mother would be very tender on these occasions. "Don't worry," she consoled me. "What does he know? You're really a very nice boy." But Granny just asked, "And then what?"

"Well, he was rude to me, Granny, so I was rude back!"

She shook her head slowly. "What is the connection?" I had no answer, of course. Then came the words I dreaded most to hear from her lips. "You're such a bright boy. Tell me, what does his being rude have to do with what you say or do?"

"But Granny," I said, "he's impossible to get along with!"

"There is only one person in the world you can hope to control," she replied drily, "and that is yourself. Work on how *you* respond. Otherwise you are like a rubber ball: he throws you against the wall and you bounce back."

Of course, just hearing this kind of advice does not necessarily help much. If my coach had merely said, "You don't hold the racquet right," it would not have improved my tennis game. I would have objected, "Show me how I'm holding it wrong and how to hold it right!" What made Granny a consummate teacher is that she could always show me how to solve my problems: by working on my own mind.

ॐ

One of the major difficulties in learning to train the mind is that it is so hard to stand back and see our thoughts clearly. The mind — everybody's mind — is a vast factory, producing a continuous stream of thoughts of every description: a wisp of anxiety followed by a strong desire; then another anxiety, a palpable fear, two or three irrelevant memories, a surge of anger . . . the assembly line goes on and on. Most of us see ourselves as nothing more than the product of these thoughts. That is where the danger lies.

This mind factory reminds me of the cotton factories in British India. Madras has produced fine cotton for centuries, but when new manufacturing techniques were introduced they slowed production considerably. We Indians had to wait a good while before getting an opportunity to buy. When the finished product finally appeared in the store, one table would have a small stack of fine cotton, called *hanava,* and another table would boast a huge pile of rejects. There was a fascinating variety of these. I remember picking up a nice-looking shirt that wrinkled up later like a prickly pear. When my laundryman tried to wash it, disastrous things happened.

Most of the products of our mind factory, too, are rejects. The reason is simple: out of ignorance, or under the banner of some naive notion of freedom, we refuse to supervise production. Our philosophy is free enterprise, "make whatever you like," and that is what rejects are all about.

Anger makes a good example. All of us know people who are accident-prone: on their way to deliver a few words in front of the Garden Club they drop their pen, and when they bend over to pick it up, their feet get tangled in the microphone cord and down they go in a heap. It can be tragic. Yet how many more of us are anger-prone! All it takes is thinking angry thoughts a thousand times, enough to make anger a reflex. Then we are capable of flying off the handle and saying and doing unkind things with no provocation at all. This is merely a case of the machines of the mind taking over and running *us,* which is what conditioning means. Such a simple diagnosis of a terrible problem! But it points the way to a solution, for it locates the answer in the mechanics of the mind.

If you go on turning out the same kind of reject thought over and over, the machinery becomes conditioned: it begins to specialize in manufacturing that particular type of thought. Then, just as the machines in a garment factory might stamp out the same pattern of shirt from several different fabrics, the machines in your mind factory will keep on producing the same pattern of thought. Whatever you put in, you get the same old response: anger, hostility, suspicion, jealousy, whatever the mind has been habituated to turn out.

When we see someone reacting like this we say, "That's the kind of person he is." What we should say is "That's the kind of mind he has" — or, more accurately, "That's the kind of thinking his mind does." He has let his mind factory turn out the same response again and again, and now it produces automatically.

&

Not only could my tennis coach see clearly what a player was doing wrong, he had a systematic method for showing how to set things right. We can do the same with the mind. Through personal experience, I have developed a method for introducing quality control in the mind: the eight points described at the end of this book, which I have followed in my own life.

I do not claim to have made these points up. In fact, part of their appeal is that they appear in all the world's great spiritual traditions. But because of my Western training, the methods I present are not particular to any country, culture, or religion; they have been well worked out for modern times. They comprise a program anyone can follow for teaching the mind to be calm and kind, just the way my coach would have presented it: one, two, three, four, five . . .

First and foremost comes meditation, because through meditation we can actually lay our hands on the machinery of the mind. This is imperative, for the mind factory is already in full production: daytime, swing shift, even graveyard. Thoughts love to work through the weekend without pay, and they never call a strike. "We just get into a rhythm," they would explain, "and we can't stop." With this powerful internal machinery always running, it is crucial to have a supervisor on the job.

The method of meditation I teach involves sitting quietly with eyes closed and going slowly, in the mind, through the words of an inspirational passage that appeals to you deeply. It might be a prayer, or a poem from one of the great mystics, or a piece of scripture from any of the world's religions. This method has several direct effects on the quality of thinking. To begin with, it gives the mind's machinery better raw material. When you sit quietly every morning with your eyes closed, concentrating completely on words that embody your highest ideals, you are giving your mind thoughts of the purest quality to work with during the day. A perfect example is the opening of the Buddha's Twin Verses, taken from the Dhammapada:

All that we are is the result of what we have thought: we are formed and molded by our thoughts. Those whose minds

are shaped by selfish thoughts cause misery when they speak
or act. Sorrows roll over them as the wheels of a cart follow
the hooves of the bullock that draws it.

All that we are is the result of what we have thought: we are
formed and molded by our thoughts. Those whose minds
are shaped by selfless thoughts give joy when they speak or
act. Joy follows them like a shadow that never leaves them.

When it comes to substituting high quality for low,
however, no passage could improve on the inspiring
prayer of Saint Francis of Assisi:

> Lord, make me an instrument of thy peace.
> Where there is hatred, let me sow love;
> Where there is injury, pardon;
> Where there is doubt, faith;
> Where there is despair, hope;
> Where there is darkness, light;
> Where there is sadness, joy.
>
> O Divine Master, grant that I may not so much seek
> To be consoled as to console,
> To be understood as to understand,
> To be loved as to love;
> For it is in giving that we receive;
> It is in pardoning that we are pardoned;
> It is in dying to self that we are born to eternal life.

One reason this kind of training is so effective is that it
uses the same machinery that gives the mind its immense
power. For meditation to work, you don't have to reason
over, reflect on, question, or answer the words you are
meditating on — in fact, if you do, you are letting the mind
do its own thing again, letting it produce whatever it
wants. Instead, all you have to do is try to give complete
attention to one word at a time, and bring the mind back
when it wanders. If you are giving a word your best attention, its meaning cannot help sinking in. Anything else actually keeps the meaning from penetrating.

If this sounds easy, try it. The whole factory will rebel.
For a long, long time you will feed the words in and the

machines will spit them right back at you. The mind will insist on producing its own things, thinking its own thoughts: everything from little distractions (such as what you need to do that day) up to major crises, when you cannot get the mind out of a vicious circle of hostility or craving. To focus on the words of the Buddha or Saint Francis, you need to slow down the frantic pace of the thinking process so that you can pay attention to one thought at a time.

Somehow, in our modern civilization, we have acquired the idea that the mind is working best when it runs at top speed. Yet this is not true even with assembly-line production. A racing mind lacks time even to finish a thought, let alone to check on quality. It just churns out whatever it can, the more the better, and the faster it runs the more likely it is to overheat, jam, and even shut down and have to be restarted. Slowing down the mind means not only achieving better quality but actually getting more done. A smooth-running flow of thought saves a lot of wear and tear on the nervous system, which means more vitality and resilience in the face of stress.

Until you experience it, this may sound like the kind of control that takes the joy out of living. But if I may say so, most thoughts are neither joyful nor necessary. It took me many years of meditating to make this discovery. Anxious thoughts — who needs them? Worry — better off without it. Resentments — why ask? Quite a host of our troubles, if you stop to think about it, are due to thinking too much.

Let me hasten to make clear that I am not saying we should throw the machinery of the mind away. I have been meditating for decades, and I assure you, my mind has never functioned better. But I use it when I want it; it does not use me. My thoughts have to come by invitation. Most thoughts are gate-crashers, you see; that is my objection to them. And negative emotions like anger and resentment not only come without an invitation, they crash the party early and eat up all the food. When the proper guests arrive the plates are empty, the chairs are upside down, and the place is in chaos. Quality control simply means that when thoughts come you can say, "May I see your invitation?" If they don't have one, you say, "Excuse me, but this party is not for you."

Meditation, then, is bringing your attention back to quality thoughts, over and over and over. When distracting thoughts intrude, you simply return your attention to the words of the passage. But don't try to evaluate each thought that arises while you are meditating; you will find yourself lost in a forest of distractions. Instead, teach your mind that during its period of meditation it has one job and one job only: to keep to the plans laid out by Saint Francis. Anything else, however fascinating, is out of order. With practice your mind will take to this job rather well, and reminders of your meditation passage will come to your mind at crucial times throughout the day.

In some ways, training the mind is very much like training a dog. When we take our dog Ganesha for a walk in the countryside, the moment he sees a calf or a deer he wants to jump the fence and take off after it. We call, "Come back, Ganesh," and Ganesha comes back halfway. But the old pull remains, and as soon as we look the other way Ganesha is off again. We repeat: "Come back!" It may take a dozen patient repetitions, but Ganesha finally settles down and trots amiably by our side.

It is the same with the mind. When you sit down to meditate, a little calf of a distraction slips barely noticed past the edges of your consciousness. Suddenly, instead of repeating the words of your meditation passage, you find yourself going over what you plan to tell that client you are seeing for lunch. You make a resolution: "I'm not going to think about her now! I've got time blocked out for that when I get to work." But your mind says, "Listen, I've thought of a new slant. If you want me to hold it till nine-thirty, you're taking a pretty big chance. Why not just make a note of it? Here, take this down . . ." And you're off.

Five minutes later, after replaying several versions of luncheon appointments past and future, you suddenly remember Saint Francis. "Between rehashing yesterday and planning for today," you exclaim in exasperation, "what's the point in even trying to meditate?" Don't get discouraged; just keep calling your mind back to the words of the inspirational passage. This is one of the most satisfying principles in meditation: you don't have to concern yourself with distractions; all you need do is try to keep your attention completely on the passage — and practice, practice, practice.

When distractions come, they can knock on the door of the mind as if they were bent on breaking it down. We get annoyed and open it with a bang, demanding, "Don't you know I'm trying to meditate? Who do you think you are?" That's exactly what the distraction wants. It grins and says, "Thanks, boss. That's just what I wanted to talk to you about. Have you got a minute?" It stands there with its foot in the door, and we are too polite to walk away.

Resisting distractions only strengthens them by giving them your attention. Instead of struggling with distractions when they come, simply give more attention to the words on which you are meditating: "It is in giving that we receive; it is in pardoning that we are pardoned. . . ." The more attention you give to the passage, the less there will be for anything else. As your concentration improves, the disturbance from distractions will become less and less. After a while you may not be aware of the distraction at all; your mind will be absorbed in the words of Saint Francis.

ข**ๅ**

This sounds like plain, dull work, so let me show you some of its very useful applications.

For one, everybody knows how painful it is to keep thinking about an unpleasant memory. Actually, the problem is not the memory but the fact that we cannot stop thinking about it. We can spare ourselves the agitation by withdrawing the mind from that memory completely.

Is this just playing Pollyanna — hiding from problems and pretending they are not there? Perhaps it would be, if worrying could help. But worrying never helps. If you really have to think about the past to solve a problem, think about it, draw your conclusions, and then drop it; don't let your mind run on, turning out the same unproductive stuff. Meditation can help solve such problems in other ways, too, by going to their root; I shall say more about that later. Here I am simply talking about learning to drop at will those haunting specters from the past that nag, "You're no good, you're no good," or push us unwillingly into the same old situations again and again.

Take resentment, for example. Resentment is nothing more than compulsive attachment to a set of memories. If you could peek through the window of the mind factory when you feel resentful, you would see the production line turning out the same emotion-charged memory over and over: "He did that to me in 1983, he did that to me in 1983 . . ." You are dwelling on something that took place in the past — or, more likely, on how you misunderstood that event and reacted to your misunderstanding. When you keep pumping attention into an event in this way, even a limp little memory gets blown up into a big balloon of hostility. If you can withdraw your attention, the balloon is deflated. There is nothing more to it.

Once my young nieces brought home a box of balloons and blew them up until our living room was full of them. It was great fun until one of the balloons burst, leaving only a shred of rubber. Similarly, when you stop pumping up a resentment, there is nothing left to cause trouble. Burst balloons can bring tears to children's eyes, but a burst resentment floods the heart with relief and love.

Brooding on memories not only serves no earthly purpose, it can go on until your mind is so filled with balloons that there is no room for the joy of living. But through meditation, by withdrawing your attention from distractions, you can train your mind to the point where no memory can upset you or drive you into compulsive action.

This is not amnesia. Your memories are still there in the file if you need them. What is lost is their emotional charge. The door of the past may still open and let an old memory swagger in, clanking its chains in your face and expecting you to climb under your desk and hide. But with a trained mind you will be able to sit there calmly, watching the show with an expression of infinite tolerance. When it is finished you can clap politely and say, "Very professional performance. Now, if you're quite through, I have things to do." The poor memory, not used to this kind of treatment, will duck its head and slink out, leaving not a trace of disquiet in your mind.

There is no exaggeration in this. Through many years of practice you can gain such command over your thinking process that if there is a spurt of hostility toward someone you have only to look at your mind and say "No." The hostility will wither. If resentment creeps in you can say "Please leave," and it will go. That is why, after more than forty years, I still catch myself thinking every day, "There is nothing like meditation!"

Training the Mind

RECENTLY MY WIFE AND I took some friends to San Francisco. The day was beautiful, bright and sunny without being uncomfortably hot, and the air was so clear that we had a full view of the Berkeley hills across the bay. As we crossed the Golden Gate a light breeze was blowing, making the water dance with sunlight.

We went straight to the Marina for a walk. I like to watch sailboats under full, colorful sail, and I enjoy the birds — sea gulls, curlews, and the unabashed pigeons that come and look you straight in the eye as if to say, "What have *you* brought for me to eat?" But what especially fascinated me was a number of people running around the Marina lawns, stopping in turn at certain places to do a specific routine: jumping, bending, twisting, stretching. The city had put up exercise stations, it seems, so that men and women could come there regularly to keep fit. You start at Station 1 and do the recommended exercises; then you jog on to Station 2, and so on around the field.

I watched one man do an exercise over and over — flexing and extending first one leg, then the other, again and again and again. I felt sure he had an objective in view; probably he was trying to develop certain muscles for a particular sport.

On the far side of the park, some other fellows were apparently trying to push their car to get it started. "They're just doing their stretches," my wife explained.

With so many runners in this country today, we are familiar with scenes like this. Everybody knows about warming up and cooling down and all the rest. But what most people do not realize is that the mind needs to be stretched too. The purpose of warm-up exercises is to keep the body supple so that you do not strain a muscle. If you go out to run when your body is stiff, every muscle will complain; the real race will be to see which one quits first. Similarly, if you try to work with difficult people — including yourself — when your mind is stiff, you are bound to get tense. Your patience may snap; your digestive organs may go on strike. You may have trouble sleeping at night, and if you do succeed in falling asleep you may not want to get up. Meditation is warm-up exercise for the mind, so that you can jog through the rest of the day without getting agitated or spraining your patience.

At each station on the Marina course, I noticed, the signs not only give instructions in an exercise, they also explain its purpose. "Do this to strengthen the muscles of the back." "This will help to flatten your stomach." Just as there are certain exercises for toning a particular set of muscles, there are special exercises for developing a fit personality. Every provocation is an exercise for developing patience; every opportunity to retaliate offers a chance to harness your passions. The question is the same as in a physical fitness program: how much do you want to get in shape?

Every difficulty during the day can be looked on as an exercise station like those on the Marina. Often the breakfast table is Station 1. It has certain mental bars and rings and stands, and just as the athlete I saw was strengthening his leg muscles, you can use life's inevitable annoyances to strengthen your love, patience, and respect.

Most breakfast trials arise from being rigid about what we like and dislike — which, incidentally, is the source of much of the agitation in personal relationships. "I don't like that job, I don't like her, I don't like this, I don't like that." Listen to people and you can hear this refrain everywhere.

If we live alone, we may not hear these notes of pique as the ego expresses its little preferences. But breakfast with family or friends is a different story. You like your coffee strong; she likes hers light. He wants eggs and you can't stand them. Isn't there a king in an English nursery rhyme who turned his kingdom upside down to get breakfast *his* way? "No one, my dear, would call me a fussy man; I simply like a bit of butter for my royal slice of bread." If the ego could be king, most of us would sound too much like this to be attractive. Artistry in living begins with learning to be flexible for the sake of those around us.

For most people, the place of work is Station 2 — office, factory, school, wherever you have to work with other people. There too the story is the same, for you don't leave your dislikes at home. When you walk in, the receptionist is clipping her fingernails at her desk again, and somebody is sharpening his pencil with an unnerving rhythm. Even tiny things can irritate: "Why does he have to sharpen his pencil like that? Why does she have to clip her fingernails *now?*" I am not exaggerating. When likes and dislikes are allowed free rein, any little thing can be upsetting; clicking nail clippers can sound like castanets. What an exercise for training attention! If you can get your mind off the Spanish dancing and completely onto your work, the distractions will disappear and you will find you have reached a new level of willpower, concentration, and flexibility.

With practice we can learn not to be bothered by life's petty trials, which leaves us the vitality and resilience we need when the big trials come. We even have staying power left over when we go home. Then we can say, "Sure, the office was terrible. That's just why I want to show you how much I love you." Anyone who can say that will be cherished everywhere. Nothing can disturb such a person's love or loyalty.

A friend of mine worked for years as a machinist. Machine tool technology can bring together very disparate individuals, and Ed found the differences trying. I reminded him, "Differences are only natural where people work together. You don't come from the same place or share the same family background. You had different parents, grew up with different values, faced different challenges. You shouldn't be surprised to discover you have conflicting ways of doing things."

I called up what little I knew about machine work. "Don't you have a polisher there?" I asked.

"Sure," said Ed. "Several of them."

"When you go off to work tomorrow, don't tell Laurel you are going to fabricate flywheels. Say, 'I'm off to do more polishing.' That is one function of the workplace that people never think of: it is a place where you can smooth and polish the rough spots of your personality."

"Smooth and polish," of course, is a nice way of saying there is going to be abrasion. This is not pleasant, I agree. But it can be highly artistic once you get the hang of it. Isn't lens grinding an accomplished art? A skilled worker can polish a piece of glass into a precise, powerful lens. Similarly, meditation can shape and polish personality into a lens that concentrates and magnifies the greatest of human resources.

With everybody at work needing more polish, of course, the day is full of opportunities for exercise. If you want to see how your meditation is going, measure yourself against this course. You can draw up a checklist — Station 2, the switchboard operator; Station 3, the staff meeting; and so on through the day. When you make a harmless statement and your boss gets irritated, that is an exercise station. She doesn't want to be unkind, but the teeth of her mind are on edge. Snapping back at her is like lying down in front of the exercise sign and saying, "I can't do it!" You lose the opportunity to strengthen a particular muscle. If the exercise is stressful, that is precisely because you need it. As in physical fitness, you just work on it a little; soon you will be doing it effortlessly.

To judge from the best-seller lists, millions of people today are interested in slimming down parts of their anatomy. One advertisement proclaims, "A flat stomach is beautiful!" For me, a flat ego is beautiful. A big ego has sharp angles and corners that stick out everywhere; we cannot get near such a person without getting hurt. But when you have reduced the rough bulges of self-centeredness to the bare minimum, you can jog through the day without stress or effort. When you come to an exercise you do it smoothly and gracefully, bounce to your feet, and run on.

The more we indulge our personal demands, on the other hand, the fatter the ego grows. This fierce drive of self-will—"*I* must get what *I* want, *I* must have *my* way" — makes us insecure, disrupts our relationships, alienates others, and lowers our self-esteem. Anybody who expects people to let him have his own way is going to have a miserable time in personal relationships. Even where beauty is concerned, I would say it is much more important to have a flat ego than to flatten any part of the body.

The exercise for reducing the ego is simple: put the welfare of others before your own. Pay more attention to their needs. In other words, go against self-will. Isn't that what reducing means? After all, if you have put on extra pounds through overeating, you don't expect to lose weight by eating more. You do the opposite. Similarly, when your needs conflict with those of others, the exercise is to try to look on their needs as your own. Often you will discover that it costs you nothing to yield — except, of course, your ego's gnashing of teeth. Let them gnash. You are growing, gaining great strength for facing challenges more worthy of your steel.

I always try to make clear that this does not mean making yourself a doormat, saying yes to anything people say or do. Putting the welfare of other people first is not the same as doing whatever they want. If someone close to you wants something that is in no one's best interests, or something which you feel is wrong, it is necessary to say no, respectfully but firmly. The point of this exercise is not to weaken good judgment but to reduce self-will: to become more sensitive to others' needs and less insistent about our own, which often turn out to be only rigid likes and dislikes in disguise.

For the adventurous, here is a special exercise for trimming away self-will: don't spend time only with people you like. Now and then, take a walk with someone you dislike; take that person to lunch. And don't always talk to the same people at work; cultivate relationships with everybody. You will be expanding your consciousness, pushing the frontiers of your world outward.

In every fitness program, of course, it is stick-to-itiveness that counts. You get nowhere if you exercise by fits and starts. Don't go out one day and do a lot of exercises, then get depressed the next day, go to bed, and skip the program completely. Keep on exercising, whether it feels good or not. That is how you develop a fit will and a svelte, attractive personality.

CHAPTER 4
Juggling

SOME TIME AGO, while visiting Ghirardelli Square in San Francisco, I saw an intelligent, imaginative street performer who billed himself as "one-man vaudeville." Everything he did I enjoyed, because it was so applicable to the training of the mind. Only in this case it was the hands that had been trained, which is much easier to understand.

This man was an excellent showman. He knew how to drum up business and draw in a lot of people who were wandering aimlessly about. Then, when he had a captive crowd, he started juggling — first with only one ball. "Everybody can do this," he assured us. "This is how you start juggling, with one ball."

And all of us said to ourselves, "Yeah, we can do that. Anybody can do that."

Next he started in with two — step by step, without frightening any would-be jugglers. And I said to myself, "Yeah, we can do that too."

Then he started two with one hand. The audience began to get thoughtful.

If I may make a confession, I was particularly interested in all this for a rather personal reason. When I was in high school I was a good student, and I didn't like some of the remarks made by other boys to the effect that books were all I was good for. So I decided to learn to do something that nobody else could do. I looked about and cudgeled my brain — "Hey," I said, "nobody is a juggler!"

I went to my grandmother and asked, "What would you say if I learned to juggle?"

"As long as it doesn't take time from your studies," she said, "it's all right with me."

So whenever I got a few spare minutes, I would take out a lemon . . . and then, after a while, two lemons. It was difficult. You have to time the toss well and then receive it well; the rhythm has to be just right and your concentration cannot waver. But I went on practicing, and to my amazement I succeeded. It was a great day when I went to Granny and said, "Would you like a surprise?" I started in with my lemons, and her eyes glowed with admiration.

That glow was so precious to me that I added another lemon. Try juggling with three lemons; you'll see how difficult it is. But through perseverance and nothing more, I succeeded.

This time I called in my mother also. "Both of you sit down," I announced. "You are about to see a really professional performance." I don't know who applauded more enthusiastically, my mother or my grandmother.

Now, it happened that at school gatherings, whenever everybody was hard pressed for entertainment, someone would ask me, "Wouldn't you like to recite 'The boy stood on the burning deck'?" This time I was ready for them. The next time the occasion arose I replied, "No, nothing intellectual. Real lowbrow stuff for me." I took out my lemons and started in, and I don't think I've ever seen a high school crowd so stunned.

That explains one of the reasons why I was so interested in this man's performance in Ghirardelli Square. But where I had started with A and ended with B, this man went from A to Z. Some of the things I saw him doing I couldn't believe. He would be juggling and would suddenly pass his hand right through the rain of balls, or pluck one out and toss it up behind his back. Then he would start juggling with an eggplant, a bowling ball, and a fresh egg. If you haven't juggled, the impossibility of this may escape you. To be able to juggle—or so I had always thought—you have to have objects of equal weight. Only then can your timing be good. Besides, if there is any kind of collision between a bowling ball and an egg, the result can be humiliating. But though we watched and held our breath, the catastrophe never occurred.

The climax was stupendous. First he brought out four empty beer bottles and placed them carefully on the carpet. Then he balanced an ordinary wooden chair on top of the empty bottles. I thought he was going to say, "Don't you like the way I can balance this chair?" But instead he climbed onto the chair, stood up precariously, took out two balls and an apple, and started juggling. We all thought that was the limit; but there was more. While juggling he would catch the apple and take a bite — all in rhythm — and then send it back into the fray. He did this until the whole apple had disappeared into his mouth.

Now, if I had asked, "How did you ever learn to do all this?" he might have replied, "You started too. You just didn't finish." In other words, if I had dropped out of school and juggled for hours every day instead of reading Shakespeare and Shaw, I too probably could have learned to stand in Ghirardelli Square and do what he was doing. It is essentially a question of practice — and of where you choose to put your time.

What that young man learned to do with his body, you can learn to do with your mind. With diligent practice, you can learn to stand atop old, unwanted habits of conditioned thinking and juggle gracefully with anything life places in your hands. There is no mystery about this, no magic to it. You simply start by practicing with one or two small things.

This kind of juggling begins not with eggs and egg-plants but with likes and dislikes. This is only for the adventuresome, but it makes an excellent test of spiritual awareness. Can you change your likes at will? When it benefits someone else, can you turn a dislike into a like? If you can, you have really made progress.

The reason is simple. The basis of conditioned thinking

is the pleasure principle: "Do what brings pleasure, avoid what brings pain." To act in freedom, we have to unlearn this basic reflex. We need to learn to enjoy doing something we dislike, or to enjoy not doing something we like, when it is in the long-term best interests of others or ourselves.

This is not an exotic idea. We set limits to the pleasure principle every day, largely because as human beings, we have the capacity to look beyond immediate gratification to something more important. Every good athlete understands this; so does a mother staying up to comfort a sick child. This precious capacity is called discrimination, the ability to distinguish between immediate pleasure and real benefit, and I shall have a lot to say about it in the pages to come.

Conditioning, then, comes down to being dictated to by our likes and dislikes. And the first place we encounter likes and dislikes is when the senses are involved: with all the things we love (or hate) to taste, see, listen to, smell, or touch. Highbrow or low, almost everyone holds on tightly to sensory likes and dislikes. But by learning to toss them up and juggle with them freely, turning a like into a dislike or a dislike into a like as the occasion demands, we gain much more than a party skill: we get a precious handhold on the workings of the mind.

When you say no to a calorie-laden treat, or yes to a restaurant you dislike but your partner really enjoys, you are learning to juggle with your likes and dislikes in food. When you say no to music that stirs up old passions, you are juggling with your hearing. You can do this with all the senses. In the films you see, the books and magazines you read, the television shows you look at, the conversations you participate in — everywhere you can learn to say, "No, this doesn't help anybody, so I won't do it; yes, this is beneficial, so I'll do it with enthusiasm."

This is the way I trained my own mind, and I recommend it to everyone with a sense of adventure. Sometimes you have to grit your teeth, but the fierce thrill of mastery is exhilarating. It is not possible to convey what freedom comes when you can juggle with your likes and dislikes at will.

We can get so caught up in our subtle maze of likes and dislikes that we temporarily lose our sense of direction. As Spinoza says, we mistake our desires for rational decisions. We tell ourselves, "I like this, so I do it. I don't like that, so I don't bother with it. What other basis is there for making a decision?" What we really mean is, "I'm in a car that turns of its own accord. I can't help going after things I like, and I can't help avoiding things I dislike." We have only to look at ourselves with detachment to see how much of our daily routine amounts to little more than going round and round in the same old circles.

There is real truth to an old saying: "The immature person does what he likes; the mature person likes what he does." In the newspaper recently, three or four persons on the street were asked what quality they most admired in a friend. I would have liked to surprise the interviewer by saying, "Flexibility in likes and dislikes." Its beneficial effects are immediate and wide-ranging: on our health, because it gives us a shield against stress; on our emotional stability, because now we hold the steering wheel in our own hands; on our relationships, because on most issues we can give easily, without rancor.

Flexibility can be practiced everywhere, starting with food. My friend Brian, who wrote the nutrition section of the *New Laurel's Kitchen,* once told me that the thorniest problem in the whole field of human nutrition is helping people to change their eating habits. Even when they know their health demands it, change is almost impossible, simply because likes and dislikes about food can be so rigid.

Suppose, for example, that you have been looking forward to Belgian waffles for breakfast. When you come to the table and find blueberry pancakes, you feel so disappointed! There is nothing shabby about blueberry pancakes, but you have been dreaming of Belgian waffles smothered with fresh strawberries and gleaming with a crown of whipped cream. Many a breakfast table has been the scene of a small Waterloo over just such an incident. But on the spot you can start practicing flexibility, juggling waffles and pancakes. If you have children, a few scenes like this will convey a great deal. They may not say anything, but they will gradually absorb a precious secret about life: being able to change your likes and dislikes means you are always free to enjoy.

If I may say so, I think this skill is much harder to learn for those of us who grew up in countries where food is very highly spiced. Just as children in this country go to the ice cream parlor after school, we used to go to a mango tree — even when the fruit was not yet ripe. To South Indians, green mangoes have a complex appeal: partly sour, partly sweet, partly pungent. And we had our rituals about how they should be eaten. One, at least for boys in my village, was that you should get your mango without climbing the tree. You have to take a little stone, sharpen it, and knock the fruit from the branch — and it is not supposed to touch the ground, either; you have to catch it as it falls. Then you season your prize liberally with red pepper and salt — everybody brought his own from home — and enjoy it right on the spot. I might add that our red pepper is not the civilized cayenne pepper you get in this country. Kerala peppers are flaming hot.

This is the kind of food South Indians enjoy. It should burn. Just imagine! So when somebody has been eating this way morning, noon, and evening for twenty or thirty years, it is almost impossible to change to milder food. Yet it can be done.

Some years ago a distinguished Indian scholar visiting this country was drawing me out about the life I was leading here. "I hope," he said earnestly, "that you have made arrangements for getting Indian food."

"Oh, no," I said. "Now I eat food without chilies or spices, and with very little salt."

He shivered visibly. "How horrible!" He couldn't know that for the passing pleasures of red pepper and green mango, I had bought a lasting joy.

⁊&

One of the first things I learned from Mahatma Gandhi was that training the palate is a powerful aid in training the mind. The reason is simple: you get at the mind through the senses, and taste is a double sense. Ask a gourmet: when something appeals to the palate, flavor and aroma are combined. So for those who want the taste of freedom, I am going to make a rather unpleasant suggestion. When you have the opportunity to eat some special delicacy which you like very much, choose instead to ask for something nourishing that you don't particularly enjoy. Try it: you won't like it. At first it may make your skin crawl. Then why do I suggest it? Because even two or three experiments like this bring a heady sense of self-mastery. If you get hooked, you will see for yourself how much freer your life becomes.

Every day brings opportunities to practice this, as I can illustrate with another personal example. In India, as you may know, we use many kinds of vegetables in curries, but we generally don't serve vegetables raw. A tossed green salad is just a pile of leaves to us, and the only people in India who eat leaves are characters in our ancient epics who have been exiled to a forest or have taken vows of mortification. When I came to this country, consequently, I had some difficulty in taking to salads. My body needed their nourishment, but my mind did not understand that; I had to teach it. Today I probably eat more salad than half a dozen of you together, and I enjoy it immensely.

But the challenges didn't end there. The first time I tried asparagus, for example, it really tasted like grass to me. I might as well have been eating plankton. My mind objected strenuously. "This isn't food!"

I remember picking up the *San Francisco Chronicle* in those days and seeing a gourmet columnist announce with joy, "The asparagus season has arrived!" It struck fear into my heart. I asked myself, "Will it claim me for its own someday?"

"Asparagus is full of valuable nutrients," the columnist wrote. "So what?" my taste buds demanded. "What about us?" I thought they had a point. To get nutrients into the blood, you first have to get them past the taste buds. Mine stood there like armed sentinels, saying "No!"

Yet now — it is a real tribute to my mind — I eat so much asparagus that at my next physical examination my blood may prove green. Friends buy it for me by the crate. When I went to the store a few days ago, I was introduced to the produce man as "the man who eats all that asparagus!" He was duly impressed.

There is no struggle in this any longer. I don't face a plate of asparagus with a sense of conflict, and I don't force it down either; I enjoy it. With lots of nutrients and so few calories, it is excellent for my body's needs.

You can juggle with likes and dislikes about work in the same way.

Whatever the job, all of us feel a natural desire to work at what we like, in the manner we like, with the people we like, and at the times we like. This happens so quietly that we seldom notice that our little preferences are making choices for us. Only as my meditation deepened did I begin to see that I was drifting toward doing things I liked and away from doing things I didn't like, without my even being aware of what was happening. Discrimination dawned with the insight that I was rarely acting in freedom.

One secret I learned was to try to see myself as someone else would. That enabled me to see with clearer eyes what I was avoiding and why. When you look at your life in this way, you soon find opportunities to work in circumstances that may not be to your liking — perhaps even with people you don't like — but where your help will benefit others. In such situations, most of us not only lose our patience, our concentration, and our good manners; often we lose our skill as well. That is the challenge. If you can only do well at jobs that are fun, what is special about that?

Again, let me illustrate from my own experience. For most of my life I have luxuriated in literature. I fell in love very young with the best from both English and Sanskrit, two of the richest literary traditions in the world, and I must have memorized thousands of lines of poetry; that was the extent of my passion. I carried Palgrave's *Golden Treasury* in my pocket wherever I went, and during the summer I used to go up to a spectacular, secluded spot we called the Glittering Rocks, where mica-sprinkled stones rose above the headwaters of our river, and recite aloud the whole of Gray's "Elegy" or the *Rubáiyát of Omar Khayyám*. I mention this just to give an idea of the love I poured into literature, which I haven't lost even today.

Yet today, although I still sit up reading until late at night, the one thing I almost never touch is literature. Everything is medicine, science, political essays, economic analyses — with one or two exceptions, the most forbidding stuff. Sometimes it turns out that the writer has little to say and little interest in saying it well either. At times like these, despite all its training, my mind still complains. "I don't like this!" it says. "You have a volume of Maugham short stories on your shelf; can't we read one of those for a while, just for a break?"

"Like it or not," I tell my mind, "this is part of our work now. So let's see what we can learn about emotional factors in heart disease." My mind has learned to accept this answer without groaning. It has become natural, effortless, to ignore my personal preferences when it serves the interests of the whole.

Even after years of training, I assure you, your mind will keep a few harmless likes and dislikes. That is its nature. The difference is that you no longer get compulsively attached to them. You don't lose your capacity to enjoy life's innocent pleasures; you lose the capacity to get caught in them like a fly in amber. In other words, you always have a choice. You can view your predilections with a detached eye, and you can change them, if necessary, as easily as you change your shirt.

Without this flexibility, likes and dislikes can become rigid and ingrained. Strong likes and dislikes lead to strong passions, which are an open gateway to anger. Just contradict someone with rigid opinions and see what happens; you could insert a thermometer into his mind and watch the temperature rise. Don't you talk about a "hot temper"?

A really angry person has a "temp" of one hundred and four. His mind is agitated, so his attention gets scattered: he cannot listen to anybody, and he gets stirred up before he even knows what the subject is.

I have heard some good American advice for such a person: "Keep your cool." When you keep your cool, the mind does not flutter; it is still. Then you see everybody's point of view clearly. You have the understanding to help the person who is agitated with you, and if necessary, you can oppose his views without getting overheated or apologetic.

Juggling with likes and dislikes, then, is much more than learning to be flexible about the relative merits of foods or jobs or people. The real issue is freedom. Our habitual responses in small matters reflect the way we respond to life itself: the person with rigid tastes in food is likely to have rigid tastes in other fields as well. All of these hold him hostage. He is happy so long as he gets everything the way he likes it. Otherwise — which may be ninety-nine percent of the time — he is unhappy over something. He might as well be bound hand and foot.

My grandmother used to tell me, "Don't ever beg from life." Life has only contempt for people who say, "Please give me two things I like today: one in the morning, preferably just before lunch, and another about midway through the afternoon, when I start to get irritable . . . Oh, and please remember to keep everything I dislike at a convenient distance." This is panhandling, and we usually get what we deserve — disappointment, with a capital D.

We are not beggars, Granny would say; we are princes and princesses. We can learn to say to life, "It doesn't matter what you bring today. If you bring something pleasant, I will flourish; if you bring something unpleasant, I will still flourish." Once we have tasted the freedom of juggling at will with our personal preferences, we can face whatever comes to us calmly and courageously, knowing we have the flexibility to weather any storm gracefully. This is living in freedom, the ultimate goal of training the mind.

PART 2

Deeper Waters

CHAPTER 5

Learning to Swim

MY FRIENDS' CHILDREN have been learning to swim, and throughout the summer I received glowing reports about how well they were doing. At the beginning, I remember, the children themselves turned in a very different story. "Just looking at all that water makes me scared," they told me. "I'll never be able to swim!" They believed that, and they acted on it. When their parents drove them into town for lessons, there was wailing and gnashing of teeth all along the road.

Now these same children have invited me to preside over their graduation from swimming school. They look forward to coming to the pool now; they swim back and forth, play games underwater, even dive in the deep end. This did not come about overnight. It came through hard work, under the guidance of a good swimming teacher who knows just how to demonstrate the strokes and skills she wants her pupils to develop.

The transformation starts in the "kiddie pool," where drowning is difficult even if you have a talent for it. There the children learn to duck their heads under the water and hold their breath. They learn to blow bubbles. They hold on to the side and learn to kick.

Finally comes time for the big pool, of which they are scared stiff. This is only natural; after all, the water is over their heads. To their vivid imaginations, drowning is too distinct a possibility to ignore, lifeguard or no lifeguard. And it looks so far from one side to the other!

Partly they are persuaded into the water; partly, I suspect, they are pushed. They feel this is a monstrous unkindness. "We're land creatures," they want to argue. "Why should we learn to get along in an alien element?" That is a logical question. But after a while, through guidance and experience, they lose that fear of the water. Now they are at home in the pool.

We accept this as a natural part of a child's education. Learning to do stunts in the water is part of growing up. If we never get the opportunity to see somebody do such wonderful things in the mental world, it is mainly because our civilization offers no real facilities for training the mind. But with the right training, any of us can learn to be at home in the world of the mind, just as those children learned to be at home in the water.

Classical Indian mysticism compares the mind to a lake, which for most of us is continually lashed into waves by the winds of emotional stimulus and response. The real storm winds are four: anger, fear, greed, and self-will. One or another is generally blowing; if it's not the southerly, it's a nor'wester. As a result, the water is in a constant state of agitation. Even when the surface appears calm, murky currents are stirring underneath.

Through meditation and the other powerful allied disciplines, however, the lake of the mind can be made absolutely clear. When not even a ripple disturbs the surface, you can look into the crystal waters of the mind and see the very bottom: the divine ground of existence which is the basis of our personality.

Christian mystics call this center of personality "the Christ within." In Sanskrit it is called simply *Atman*, "Self." But the Buddha did not even go that far. He made no attempt at all to tell us what we shall see there. Always practical, he leaves the labels to us; his job is to get us to make the discovery ourselves. "You don't have to accept anybody's word for this," he would say. "Dive deep and see for yourself what you find." Despite all the words that scholars have written on this subject, we can understand this supreme discovery only when we experience it ourselves. This is the great paradox of mysticism: until you enter *nirvana,* to use the Buddha's term, you will not be able to understand what nirvana is.

We can get an intriguing clue, however, through this image of the lake of the mind, which fits well with the Buddha's concept of consciousness. On the surface level of awareness, everyone seems separate. We look different, wear different clothes, have different speech patterns, different ambitions, different conditioning. This is the physical level of awareness, below which the vast majority of us cannot see because of the agitation of the mind.

Just below the surface is the level of personal, individual consciousness, a comparatively shallow region which is easily stirred by the winds of sense impressions and emotions. The more physically oriented we are — that is, the more we identify with our bodies and feelings — the more caught up we will be in this mind-world of constantly changing forms. In this state it can be quite a chore to get close to other people; all our awareness is caught in the things that make us seem separate from them and unique. Their differences seem to keep getting in our way.

Underlying this level, largely unsuspected, is what the Buddha calls *alaya-vijnana:* "storehouse consciousness," the depths of the collective unconscious. There is only one alaya-vijnana; at bottom, everyone's unconscious is one and the same. The deeper we get, the more clearly we shall see that our differences with others are superficial, and that ninety-nine percent of what we are is the same for all.

To the extent that we can turn our back on our petty, private mind-world and learn to dive into deeper consciousness, we can free ourselves from the influence of the storms that stir up those shallow waters at the surface. At the same time, as we get deeper, we move closer and closer to other people; we feel closer to life as a whole. This, in effect, is what learning to swim in the unconscious is all about.

I have read of people who can race along on a Harley-Davidson and leap over a row of cars. This is an accomplishment, I agree. It requires daring, training, and resolution. But of what real use is it? By contrast, with that same kind of daring, you can learn to go deep-sea diving in the fathomless lake of the mind. In our contemporary world, when most people, I think, feel helplessly at sea, this is a vital gift. When you master it, your life becomes a beacon that others can follow.

The mind, of course, has been the subject of very serious study. But from the point of view of spiritual psychology, how can we expect to understand the mind by using the same methods we use to study the physical universe? The very concept of entering the unconscious while conscious is beyond the scope of our imagination. We identify ourselves with the mind, so how can we expect to study it objectively? As long as we believe we are the mind, we take for granted that we can find fulfillment by catering to its demands and living for its private satisfactions. And as long as we remain at the surface like this, we can never see through the mind clearly. We have little choice but to be tossed about like a toy boat in its fierce storms.

But we can learn a different perspective. In meditation we discover that we are not the mind. It is an inner world of its own, an environment we can learn to move through. Just as those children now go to the pool with eagerness on their faces, when I find tempests rising in the mind I have learned to swim with joy. I can dive to the bottom and bring up pearls, the infinite inner resources that are the legacy of us all. Instead of feeling threatened by adverse circumstances, I can remain calm and help to change those circumstances. Instead of moving away from difficult people I can actually enjoy their company, move closer to them, and win them over.

This vast treasury is within the reach of all. Sri Ramakrishna, one of the greatest mystics India has ever produced, sang ecstatically of what waits to be discovered at the seabed of consciousness:

> Dive deep, O mind, dive deep
> In the Ocean of God's Beauty;

If you descend to the uttermost depths,
There you will find the gem of Love. . . .

Once we have learned to dive deep in meditation, there is no end to the resources we can bring to our daily life; there is no challenge we will be unable to meet. Each morning we can descend to the depths and gather armloads of precious jewels: breathtaking gems of love and wisdom, lustrous pearls of patience and compassion. We can distribute them freely, knowing we have an infinite inheritance from which to draw every day.

All Life Is Yoga

"I TRY HARD IN MEDITATION," people some-
times tell me. "I have thirty minutes in the morning and
thirty more in the evening, and I really give it my best. But
I don't seem to be able to go deeper. What can I do?"

"If you are trying consistently to concentrate on the inspirational passage during those thirty minutes," I reply,
"you are doing very well. But if you want to dive deep,
you have to give your best during the times that you're not
meditating too. It is not only during meditation that we
make progress in training the mind, but also during the
rest of the day."

Once we get beneath the surface of the mind, we begin
to see that there is a very close connection between the
kinds of distractions we have in meditation and the kinds
of problems we face in daily living. It is these problems
that prevent us from diving into deeper levels of consciousness. They are both internal and external. They arise in the
mind, and we encounter them there in meditation; but because they shape our actions, we also encounter them
during the day in a hundred and one disguises.

Sri Aurobindo, one of twentieth-century India's most
luminous figures, has a good motto for reminding us of
this: "All life is yoga." Every moment, he means, is an opportunity for training the mind.

The explanation of this is simple. Every moment, from

the time we get up in the morning until we go to bed, we have a choice: to give our attention to ourselves, or to give it to those around us. If we indulge ourselves during the day, we should not be surprised to find strong distractions in meditation the next morning. On the other hand, if we reduce the number of things we do just to please ourselves, distractions will be fewer and concentration deeper.

I would go so far as to say that dwelling on oneself is the root cause of most personal problems. The more preoccupied we become with our private fears, resentments, memories, and cravings, the more power they have over our attention. When we sit down to meditate, we cannot get our mind off ourselves. With practice, however, we can learn to pay more and more attention to the needs of others — and this carries over directly into meditation. Less self-centered thinking means fewer distractions, a clearer mind, fewer outgoing thoughts to impede our gathering absorption as meditation deepens.

No one begins to meditate without a mind full of distractions. "The mind is restless, turbulent, powerful, violent," says the Bhagavad Gita. "Trying to control it is like trying to tame the wind." So when somebody complains to me about meditation being difficult, my only consolation is, "Just wait. It's going to get a lot harder." Gaining control over one's own mind is the most difficult task a human being can undertake. All this preliminary sparring with distractions in meditation is to prepare us for the really big fights to come, when we struggle to transform the powerful currents of negative thinking that swirl deep in the unconscious mind.

This is a miraculous achievement, but there is no miracle about how it is accomplished. It requires a lot of hard work. When your meditation is progressing well, if your mind goes into a negative mood — about yourself, about your problems, about other people, about the state of the world — you should be able to switch your attention away from the negative and focus it on the positive. By doing this over and over again, you can reach a state in which

negative thoughts cannot even appear on the scene. Then
your behavior is always kind, your words are always helpful, and your life becomes a positive influence on all.

This lofty achievement, of course, is slow in coming.
After the honeymoon with meditation is over, people often
tell me, "I have more trouble with my mind now than I did
when I started. Am I going backwards?"

"No," I reassure them. "It is possible to go sidewards in
meditation, but not backwards." Then I explain what is
probably happening. In the early stages, all of us have a
thousand little imps of distraction dancing around. As we
move into deeper levels of awareness, this number is reduced to two or three; but then they are no longer imps.
They are big, burly distractions, waiting for an opportunity to knock us to the floor.

This may sound bad, but it is really an encouraging
development. When you have a thousand imps hitting you
from all sides, how do you guard yourself? It is much better to have one big distraction right up front. It may be
Goliath, but at least you know what you are dealing with,
and you can train yourself to deal with it too.

These big fellows are not really distractions. They are
*samskara*s: deep, conditioned tendencies to particular ways
of thinking and acting, usually negative or self-willed,
which have been dug in the mind through many years of
repeating the same thought over and over.

Most of us, for example, have an anger samskara: an automatic response to want to lash out at others or ourselves
when things do not go our way. At critical moments like
these, it can be most helpful to remember that the disturbance has little to do with, say, whether someone took our
parking place or we had to wait in line at the grocery store.
Beneath every separate incident of anger, resentment,
hostility, and irritation lies a single reflex in the mind
which says, "I don't like this! Hit back."

Greed — not only for money but for material possessions, for pleasure, for power — is another root samskara in
the deeper consciousness of us all. It may show itself in

different ways, but the drive is the same: we feel in-
complete, so we try to manipulate things and people to get
what we can to fill the vacuum inside us.

As meditation deepens we begin to recognize these
ways of thinking in ourselves, and it may seem as if meditation has brought them on. I can assure you, they have
been there all along; we simply haven't noticed them.
Only as the mind begins to clear can we look down
through the glass-bottomed boat that is meditation and see
these monsters lurking below.

When we find ourselves face to face with a samskara in
meditation, there is no need to get rattled or try to run
away. This is what you have been training for. A kind of
Madison Square Garden has been rented in the mind, and
we are in the ring. Every morning's meditation begins
another round. But to win, we have to carry the fight out
of meditation and into daily living. Samskaras may origi-
nate in the mind, but they express themselves in words and
actions. To oppose them, we have to learn not to act on
them — not to do what our compulsions demand.

This is terribly difficult; otherwise, a compulsion would
not be a compulsion. But there is Job's consolation in
knowing that we cannot run away. We may want to jump
out of the ring and make for Brooklyn, but there is no
Brooklyn in the mind. The samskara is inside us; wherever
we go, it has to follow. Even if we refuse to fight, the Bhagavad Gita says, our very nature will impel us into situations where we have no choice. When we are against the
ropes with a burly samskara and cannot escape, reason and
self-respect agree: Why not make a good job of it and try
to win?

Whatever romantic notions we may have about spiritual
growth, it never really happens in a short time. Like the
Thirty Years' War, this war within goes on and on. There
is so much to transform! Naturally there come times when
the mind gets tired and complains. "Why not call it off for
a while?" This cannot be done. Once we come face to face
with a samskara in deeper consciousness, we are in the ring
with it until we win. As my grandmother used to tell me,

"The Lord will never put on your shoulders even one pound more than you can bear. But," she would always add, "you will never have to carry one pound less, either." Otherwise we would not grow.

≥▲

Eventually, we are trying to extend the influence of morning meditation until it becomes like a thread running through the day. Then there is a continuous connection between meditation and daily living. The timeless values on which we are meditating begin to transform every word and action. And in turn, meditation improves. When we try to show good will to everyone, to work harmoniously even with those from whom we differ, we find to our delight that meditation deepens swiftly.

Samskaras have a way of fogging vision so that what we want looks like what is really best, and what is right looks out of the question. In this kind of fog everyone needs a friend with clear vision who can block the path to disaster and say no. That is one function of a spiritual teacher.

In the countryside where I live there is a long road consisting mostly of bumps and potholes. On one side is what appears to be solid ground, covered by tall grass and California poppies. Actually all this growth conceals a deep ditch, which might qualify for the *Guinness Book of Records* for the number of cars, trucks, and even tractors that have fallen into it and had to be hauled out. One friend of mine got concerned about this and posted a discreet sign that said euphemistically, "Soft Shoulder." But vehicles kept buttressing the Guinness claim. After a year or so, my friend dropped the euphemisms and delicate lettering. Now there is a big sign that warns clearly, "DITCH!"

A samskara is not a soft shoulder; it is a deep ditch. If we get stuck in one — an addiction, a recurring personal problem, a compulsive relationship — we should count ourselves fortunate to be hauled out, even if the price is heavy. And if someone we know is about to fall into a ditch like this, it is not very loving to say, "Well, if I were you I'd consider changing my direction. But I don't want to infringe on your freedom of choice." It is not much of a sign of friendship just to say "Good luck!" and offer the address of a good garage. Even if the other person will not speak to us for a week or so, we should have enough love in our hearts to block his way. Then we can offer support while helping him to correct his negative samskara — not by preaching, but by our own example.

Here we encounter an interesting quirk of human nature: often the things we want most to correct in others are things we do ourselves. I hear both sides of this in my privileged role as spiritual teacher. A friend will come and confide to me, "That Eunice is so unkind! You'll never believe what she just said to me." I reply gently, "Do you remember when we met Eunice at the Bijou last month? That is just the way you talked to *her.*"

Sooner or later, the Buddha would say, the way we behave to others has to come back to us. That is the meaning of that much-misunderstood phrase "the law of karma." If we want people to be kind, the very best way is to learn to respond to others' needs exactly as if they were our own. No one likes to be treated rudely, to be rushed or belittled or ignored. Everyone appreciates patience, kindness, forgiveness, and respect.

As we practice this, we forget ourselves little by little — our problems, our little personal desires, our conveniences, our opinions — not only during the day but in meditation too. Then, when we sit down to meditate, there are no more distractions about our income tax or the letter we owe Aunt Julie. "Like bees returning to the hive," Saint Teresa of Avila says beautifully, "which shut themselves up to work at making honey," all our thoughts gather on the words of the meditation passage and remain absorbed there, deepening our awareness for the day to come.

ba

The thread of meditation running through your day can be extended into the evening too. If you want to go forward even in your sleep, I can share a secret which I learned over a period of ardent experimentation. Have your evening meditation reasonably early so that you have time for half an hour or so of spiritual reading before you go to sleep. And choose your reading carefully. It should be positive, strengthening, and inspiring, and it should be more than just good literature or philosophy; it should be a piece of scripture which you respond to deeply, or writing stamped with the personal experience of a great mystic. Read a little, slowly and reflectively, giving the words a chance to sink deep into your consciousness. Then put the book aside, turn out the light, and fall asleep repeating your mantram: *Jesus Jesus, Rama Rama, Barukh atta Adonai,* whatever it may be. (The use of a mantram is described in the last chapter of this book.)

It may take time, but gradually this sequence of meditation, spiritual reading, and falling asleep in the mantram will become a smooth current that goes on flowing in consciousness even while you sleep. As meditation deepens, you may find you have a remarkable night life. You may hear the words of your meditation passages reverberating in your mind, or hear the mantram being sung with a kind of unearthly beauty. You may dream of what you have been reading: you may see Saint Francis, for example, in your dreams, strengthening your heart or giving some practical advice. All this can be deeply inspiring, as if you had actually been in Saint Francis's holy company or heard the words of the Shema from the lips of Moses himself.

Even the kind of night we have, then, is of our own choice. If you have been kind throughout the day, turning your back when necessary on personal likes and dislikes, and then given your best in meditation and fallen asleep in the mantram, you will go forward even while you sleep. Even in sleep we can be shaping our lives!

In this way, with meditation and daily living supporting each other, your spiritual growth will be swift and sure.

CHAPTER 7

Tremendous Trifles

THE MOVIE *MURDER BY DEATH*, a spoof with some of fiction's most famous detectives, opens with a strange scene. Alec Guinness, a favorite of mine, plays an old, blind butler who comes in with a sheaf of envelopes to which he must affix stamps. He puts the envelopes to one side, and the camera, with surrealistic flair, shows only a wide-open mouth with the tongue sticking out. Up comes the hand with the stamps one by one, and one by one the tongue licks the stamps and the hand returns to stick them to the envelopes. We hear the fist pounding lightly to make sure each stamp is secure. Then, after the entire sheaf has been gone through, the camera backs up and we see all the stamps – carefully affixed to the desk.

All of us are capable of this if we do not pay attention to little things. Don't you have a saying that if we take care of the little things, the big things will take care of themselves? It may sound trite, yet even people with the best of intentions and the soundest of plans often fail because they overlook details that turn out to matter. If you want to see someone who will succeed, watch for the rare man or woman who takes pains over each small step.

G. K. Chesterton has a book called *Tremendous Trifles*. I find that a very apt phrase. There are a large number of tremendous trifles in life. We think they are trifles until we look back and add them up; then we discover that taken as a whole, their effect has been tremendous. It is the same with spiritual growth. Most of us who are serious about training the mind try to be vigilant on major occasions; it is on little occasions that we forget. Yet it is on these thousands of little occasions that the mind is taught to be calm and kind: not instantaneously or by great leaps, but in the ordinary choices of the day.

The Buddha, the most practical of teachers, defined the wise man or woman in a thoroughly practical way: "One who will gladly give up a smaller pleasure to gain a greater joy." That is discrimination, the precious capacity to see life clearly and choose wisely. When it is understood, every choice becomes an opportunity for training the mind.

When I first started meditating many, many years ago, in the midst of an active academic life, I had difficulty finding time for it. Most of my activities were harmless enough, but they were numerous and consumed a good deal of time and energy. I read a lot of books in those days, and much of what I read I don't think was useful even for the literature classes I was teaching. I read those books because I enjoyed them and because I had been trained to believe that literature is for enjoyment. That was the appeal made by many important figures: literature for its own sake, art for its own sake.

As my meditation deepened, however, these attitudes began to change. Nothing, I realized, is for its own sake; everything is for life's sake. This one insight simplified my priorities enormously. Immediately I began to prune my activities, lining out things that made no real difference to anybody, including myself. Today, everything I do from morning meditation on — eating breakfast, going for a walk, writing, reading, even recreation — is governed by one purpose only: how to give the very best account of my life that I can in the service of all.

That is what I mean by developing discrimination. At first it was difficult to make myself put my books aside an hour earlier to make time for evening meditation. Often my mind would protest, "Can't we read just a little more?" Yet the joy that fills my life today cannot even be measured on the same scale as the pleasures I once held dear. Once we get even a taste of what meditation can do, we start looking for ways to make time for it no matter what comes in the way.

But there *are* smaller pleasures to be given up. I am not denying that on a cold morning, for instance, it is more pleasant to stay under the blankets than to get up early for meditation. The Buddha does not say to give up a small pain in favor of a greater joy; he says, "Give up a small pleasure." That is the touch that makes him such a good teacher. Pulling the blankets over your head and lying there for ten minutes more *is* pleasant, but as pleasures go it doesn't rate more than half a cent. Perhaps if you could stay under the covers forever . . . Yet even sleep loses its attraction in time; that is the nature of life. So when you are tempted to stay in bed at the expense of meditation, remember these words: "Give up a small pleasure for a lasting joy." Meditation will enhance everything in your life. It will follow you to work and make you calmer, more energetic, more creative, and more secure.

This apparently trifling difficulty of getting out of bed in the morning hides a tremendous truth. For most of us, it is a problem built up through little acts of omission. The alarm goes off and we sigh, "Oh, just five minutes more. It's six o'clock; I'll still be there for meditation at five minutes after." That is how it begins. When you go on saying "five minutes after" every day for three hundred and sixty-five days, you develop what yoga psychology would call a five-minutes-after samskara — that is, a conditioned response that is not confined just to getting up. Everywhere you go, it will be your habit to be late and to postpone.

One powerful way to deal with this samskara — in fact, with any samskara — is to do just the opposite of what it demands. This is one of the surest ways to change a bad habit. The Buddha says, "Oppose a negative wave of thought with a positive wave of thought." It is such a simple, practical, effective strategy! The problem, of course, is that it is seldom very attractive.

Sometimes, walking at the beach when the tide is coming in, I will be striding along when a wave sweeps up, making me leap like a kangaroo to escape getting soaked. But when the tide and the contours of the shoreline are right, as the water is drawn back into the ocean it surges up in a backlash and crashes head-on into the next wave. There is a big explosion, and the oncoming wave is stopped cold.

Similarly, if a negative wave whispers to you one morning, "Just five minutes more . . . let's make it five after six," send a contrary wave back. Leap out of bed, and the next morning get up at five *to* six. Tell your mind, "If you like, you can even suggest six-thirty. I will get up at five-thirty and have my meditation." After a few mornings of this, I can assure you that your mind will have nothing more to say on the subject. This is the kind of language it understands. It is because we offer no resistance that the mind gradually begins to say "Fifteen after six" and finally, "Why not seven? It's a good, round number."

"Be reasonable," your mind may object. "Does a five-minutes-late habit do anybody any real harm?" First — and I want to emphasize this — the main issue is not the five minutes; it is training the mind. But it is important to understand that the mind's habits are not merely its own affair. Generally they affect other people in unsuspected ways as we move through the day.

I am a confirmed theater-goer, for example; I enjoy good plays and good acting. And I like to get to my seat early, mostly out of courtesy, but partly because I enjoy the human drama as the audience trickles in. On one memorable occasion the curtain went up and we were well into the opening scene when a couple stumbled in and started looking for their seats, still absorbed in a heated discussion that must have begun out on the street. The gist of it was, where was the car? They had arrived at the last moment and rushed off without noticing where they had parked, and they kept on trying to settle the matter while stepping apologetically on half a row of toes. "Was it Franklin or Polk?" "Really, dear, I think it must have been

Pine." Most of us thought this was far more dramatic than the play. I was on the verge of saying, "Please go right up on the stage. If you can sing and dance too, that is all we could want."

The same sort of scene takes place at classes, meetings, everywhere. A simple remedy is to make it a habit to go places early: we avoid making people wait for us, and we avoid interrupting them once they have started. In details like these, consideration for others becomes natural to a well-trained mind.

Once you are out of bed and sitting for meditation, the mind will probably try to distract you. That is the next "tremendous trifle": tremendous because what is at issue is not whether the subject of the distraction is big or small, good or bad, but the native distractibility of the mind.

Many people, for example, sooner or later encounter a sleeping problem in their meditation. After all, it is only natural to feel sleepy when the neuromuscular system begins to relax. And if you do doze off for a minute or two, what does it matter?

This is one subject on which I give hard-boiled advice: the moment you begin to feel sleepy, draw yourself up straight and resist. A problem with sleeping in meditation does not come one fine morning in July and ask, "May I join you?" It has been inching in, little by little by little. That is why vigilance is required right from the outset. Our impulse is to let the chin drop a little, let the spine sag, allow the words of the meditation passage to get blurry around the edges. Fight that impulse by doing just the opposite. The moment you begin to feel drowsy, draw away from your back support, sit up straight, and concentrate with all your might. When this kind of resistance becomes your natural response, you can overcome the problem of sleep even if it has been going on for months.

The mind has many, many cards like this up its sleeve. Most of us have a lot of things to attend to in the morning – some of which, it is true, we could have taken care of the night before — and of course we don't want to forget to do something vital because we have run out of time and have to rush to work. "Therefore," the mind will tell us with its own peculiar brand of logic, "why not cut meditation five minutes short and get started? What difference can five minutes make?" That is one thing you should never do. Here again, when the mind advises cutting out five minutes, smile benignly and add five minutes more.

This strategy of doing the opposite of what a conditioned impulse demands works beautifully with an eating problem. Everyone feels tempted when confronted with something tasty. Even if we are not really in need of sustenance, we often go ahead and have a little extra. It is only human, you know. "Just one little piece," the mind coaxes, "three inches by two." There again, the answer is to make it *minus* three-by-two: take a smaller piece than you would have taken. The mind can really get offended by this kind of treatment, especially after many years of having its own way. But I assure you, if you stand firm on such issues the mind will come to have such respect for you that it will think several times before trying a trick like that again.

With this strategy, we are learning a most valuable skill: we are gaining the will and the detachment not to act on impulse. Where this really pays off is in personal relationships, where acting on impulse spreads from individual to individual in countless little chain reactions throughout each day. Susan receives a letter from her mother-in-law announcing a two-week visit and she gets agitated; she cannot help it. Then she comes and says something curt to us, and we take it personally and put her on our blacklist for months. Most quarrels start with just this type of misunderstanding. It is so pointless.

When someone is unkind to us, we need not take it personally. Why should we? We are not getting hurt; if anyone is hurt, it is the other person. In India we put it picturesquely: when you are unkind to your neighbor, the cosmic auditor enters a debit for unkindness against *you.*

The rule to remember here is never to react immediately. That is the purpose of training the mind in all these other tremendous trifles. Whenever a negative emotion calls, put it on hold. Do not listen to its arguments. If you wait until all the evidence is in, there usually turns out to be no need to accept its charges, which can be heavy.

I know how hard it can be to put this rule into practice. Luckily, understanding it alone can help a great deal. Back in the days when I taught on a university campus, whenever people were curt to me I would get agitated, just as everybody does. Sometimes their sharp words could be defended; often they seemed unfair. But even when I could see their point of view I used to get agitated. Then I would recall that it is always the unkind person who pays inside, and I would begin to feel sorry for them. A little compassion would come in, and once compassion comes in, the desire to retaliate goes.

Sometimes, of course, it *is* necessary to make our differences of opinion clear. But even then it is rarely the differences themselves that make for unpleasantness; it is the arrogance with which these differences are often aired. "I am right. How can *you* possibly be right?" This is an almost universal attitude. A more appropriate approach, of course, is to concede, "There is something in what you say, and there is something in what I say. Why don't we try to find this common something?" But to do this, the mind has to be taught not to go off on impulse. Reacting on impulse is just being a jukebox: someone puts in a quarter and out comes whatever outrageous song the mind wants to sing at the time.

Who wants to be dictated to by a jukebox mind? And who would let a jukebox upset him? That is a question we can always ask ourselves when adrenaline is beginning to flow. Here, a sense of humor and a sense of humility are of great help. Most people get offended easily because they have an inflated sense of dignity. But after all, if somebody does make a remark at our expense, how is our dignity affected? It is not against us that the debit entry is made. Simply by maintaining a sense of humor and humility, we can teach the mind not to get upset even when a real trial comes.

In small matters like these, gradually the mind can be effectively trained. At home, in meditation, at work, in moments of relaxation with family and friends, we can go against the conditioned caprices of the mind and gain, little by little, control of something which often seems nebulous and elusive — our own destiny.

The Forces of Life

"LIKE A BALL batted back and forth," says an ancient text called the Yogabindu Upanishad, "a human being is batted by two forces within": one, the upward drive to evolve into spiritual beings; the other, the fierce downward thrust of our past conditioning as separate, self-oriented, physical creatures.

The literal meaning of the Sanskrit here is "like a ball hit by a stick held in the hand." I don't have any idea what game the sages of ancient India had been watching, but I think tennis fits the verse perfectly. Millions of people have taken to this sport in the past few years, so it seems a natural one to use to bring this image to life.

Imagine a match between two gentlemen players who are probably among the best the game has seen: Bjorn Borg on the one side and Ivan Lendl on the other. Bjorn caught my imagination when he came out of nowhere to win the French Open at the age of eighteen, and he has been a favorite of mine ever since. I like his manner on the court, and he has a precious quality that would serve him well if he took to meditation: like Gandhi, he is at his best when things are going against him. And Ivan Lendl, who comes from Czechoslovakia, is a serious young man with some of the most powerful strokes I have seen. One athlete reportedly asked a friend of Ivan's, "I've got to play against him; what do you suggest?" The friend replied, "A bullet-proof vest."

Imagine being a tennis ball played by these two strong champions — Lendl, whose shots must travel at more than a hundred miles per hour, and Borg, who strings his racquets so taut that at night he is sometimes awakened by the *ping!* as the strings snap spontaneously under the strain. Every one of us, this ancient text says, is being played like this twenty-four hours a day back and forth between two opposing inner forces. Here are Ivan on one side of the court and Bjorn on the other, enjoying themselves immensely, yelling to each other, "Hit him for all you're worth; I'll slam the poor fellow back!"

This inner tension is our evolutionary heritage. It reflects our divided nature as human beings: partly physical, essentially spiritual, constantly pulled in two conflicting directions. If this sounds bad, it is actually quite positive. For if one of these players will not let us alone, neither will the other. Built into our very nature is an inner drive that will not let us be satisfied with living at our lowest level, governed only by biological laws. Some inner evolutionary imperative is constantly exhorting us to grow, to reach for the highest that we can conceive, as if nature itself will not let us rest with anything less than spiritual fulfillment.

Sometimes when I am waiting at the dentist's office, I like to look at the popular magazines. It doesn't matter if they are a few months old; I am always interested in their slick advertisements. Either by innuendo or by outright declaration, they are all aimed at one deep, almost universal desire: to change who we are, make ourselves somehow better — richer, smarter, more attractive, more secure, more at home with who we are.

Unfortunately, these implicit promises of Madison Avenue deal only with externals: a fragrance that the opposite sex will find irresistible, a ring that will make a relationship "last for eternity," a house so spectacular that we will want nothing more but to lounge in it all day and admire the appointments and the view. Despite their sophisticated appearance, below every advertisement like this I would like to write, "This won't change you! You'll still be the same old person. You'll still have to live with yourself as you are."

Toward the end of the second chapter of the Bhagavad Gita there is a statement so direct, so penetrating, that it should move us to question all external attempts at self-improvement: those who are always trying to satisfy their personal desires will never find peace in this life. Such people are doomed to live in turmoil and isolation. They may live in palatial homes, hop from one resort to another, or have their photograph on the covers of the weekly magazines, but they won't have peace in their hearts. Why? Because if we cannot make changes where we really want to — in our own personality — it does not matter what else we may have achieved; we won't be able to live with ourselves. We can fool all of the people some of the time and some of the people all of the time, but there is one person — ourself — who will look at us with a cold eye and say, "You ain't foolin' me! You're not changing yourself at all; you're not growing."

Often, I think, this is why active people are so active, why adventurers adventure and globetrotters trot: we do not want to stop and listen to that quiet heckler in the depths of our hearts, reminding us of our real job. This is ultimately what insecurity means; that is where a sense of inadequacy really comes from.

During the past twenty-five years, I must have heard the same refrain from hundreds of people, particularly those who are young: "I just don't like myself." The unspoken assumption is, "This is the kind of person I am, and it's what I always will be. If I have crippling fears, the best I can do is learn to live with them. If I am prone to fits of anger, people will just have to accept me as I am."

But we *can* change. No one need ever feel resigned and say, "There is nothing I can do." There is everything we can do. That is the purpose and the power of that persistent upward force within us: if we turn inward we can remake ourselves completely, modeling ourselves in the image of the loftiest spiritual ideal we can conceive.

The other day Christine was showing me some old photographs taken when the Blue Mountain Center of Meditation was in its infancy. Two or three of those young faces we had not seen for years. Others, no longer young, were as close as the path outside our window, where a group of volunteers was working diligently at patching old asphalt. To a detached eye, the contrast was most amusing. "Look at this picture," I said, "and then look out there. Where did all that hair go?" But those were only physical changes. Much more important — and deeply gratifying — were the changes I knew these friends had wrought in their thinking processes over years of meditation. Many of them had learned to transform anger into sympathy, impatience into patience, resentment into love: not perfectly, not always, but they knew how to do it, and they knew it could be done. What could be more exhilarating?

These are changes any one of us can learn to make. If you can be secure where you were insecure, selfless where you were selfish, if you can respect people around you even if they don't like you and you don't like them, then I will say with joy, "Yes. You really *have* changed." As Meister Eckhart would say, the pauper that you were is dead; the prince is born.

This rebirth is the purpose of meditation. It is a tremendous adventure, the greatest that can beckon to a human being. It tests every quality we possess, brings into play every faculty we have. It is for embarking on this supreme adventure that we have come into the world, and until we accept the challenge, we can never really rest content with anything less.

❧

One of the greatest figures of medieval India, Ramanuja, throws light on this challenge in words that should be on the walls of every school campus, every statesman's office, every home: "What we seek as our highest goal depends upon what we believe ourselves to be."

If you reflect on this brief statement, you can get lost in its manifold ramifications. Virtually all of us believe we are physical creatures, subject to biological laws. And when you believe you are a physical creature, Ramanuja says, the highest goal you can aim at has to have physical limits. You will spend your life seeking physical satisfactions. A full diagnosis of human suffering is given in just this one line.

Like everybody else, I grew up believing that I was purely physical, a collection of biochemical constituents. My friends subscribed to this belief; my learned colleagues shared it vehemently. The world we live in is based on this view; everyone takes it for granted. Even if we believe intellectually that the human being has a spiritual side, very, very few of us can conceive of ourselves without the physical, biochemical apparatus of our body and personality.

What has changed for me since then? Everything. Not two or three things but everything. Through meditation, with the help of the demanding disciplines I followed every day in the midst of a busy life, that belief in myself as a purely physical creature has fallen away completely. Today I do not look upon myself or anyone else as physical. I identify with the Self, pure spirit, the same in all.

In this realization, the body becomes no more than a kind of jacket that you wear: you take care of it as very useful, but you never once think that it and you are the same.

Imagine if you thought you were your jacket. Taking it to the cleaners would be frightful; torn pockets would be a major trauma. It sounds silly, but that is just how most of us relate to our bodies too. To a surprising extent, we live to please our body instead of having it help and serve us. We identify with it so closely that we allow it to make decisions for us and dictate how we feel about ourselves. When our body experiences a craving, we say it's a "biological necessity." If our appearance is less than perfect, we think there is something wrong with *us*.

It is from this obsessive identification with the body, I believe, that many physical and emotional problems arise. In meditation, as we learn at deeper and deeper levels that the basis of our personality is not physical but spiritual, such problems fall away. Often we do not even have to confront them. We simply go deeper, move away from the tenements of consciousness where they arise. You can leave psychosomatic problems hanging in the closet and find another home in a much safer neighborhood; they will never be the wiser. This approach is very different from the conventional wisdom of the modern world. It cannot work without meditation. For it is much more than a change in life-style; it is a transformation of thought-style.

As we absorb this higher image of who we are, many important consequences follow. When you know that you are essentially spiritual, you no longer relate to yourself as a creature to be satisfied with physical pleasures. You do not relate to others in terms of their physical appearance. You know that your worth derives from the eternal Self within you — and because this same Self lives in the hearts of all, you find it easy to relate to everyone with respect and love.

This change in personal relationships is one of the most joyful benefits of spiritual experience, yet it brings enormous responsibilities. When we see ourselves in all, detachment from our own ego is essential. Otherwise we will get emotionally entangled in other people's problems, which is just the opposite of love.

Much of my day, for example, is spent in guiding others in meditation, both by letter and in person. Often these friends bring with them burdensome personal problems. If I identified myself with my body and mind instead of with the Self, I would not be able to bear such burdens cheerfully day after day without ever feeling burned out. I would come to the dinner table and spend half an hour staring down at my plate, thinking, "What can I do to help this person out?" When we believe we are the mind, no matter what we are doing, part of the mind cannot help chewing the same problems over and over. During meditation our concentration is scattered; during the day our vitality is drained, our security is low, and our capacity to relate to people is cramped and constrained. Everything is affected.

Today, just because of this change of belief, I do not have any demands on my vitality that I cannot meet. I can face hard blows with equanimity, help others to solve the most prickly of problems with compassion and not get involved in the turmoil. And when an emergency comes up, I can write a huge check against my vitality account and know that it will not bounce. There is no magic about this; anyone can learn to do it. Such benefits give plenty of motivation to work hard at changing our image of who we are — from a separate, physical creature into a whole, loving, spiritual being.

❧

Only when I got beneath the surface of consciousness in meditation, many years ago, did I begin to see the play of forces between these two ideals, constantly pulling us toward different goals. Then I began to long more than anything else to win my freedom and escape being banged about on the court of life.

The cry of freedom has always appealed to me deeply. Even in my youngest days, Granny could always get me to change direction with just one question: "Don't you want to be free?" So today, if someone is allergic to phrases like "spiritual living," I say, "All right. Let's talk about living in freedom." Until we stop letting ourselves get knocked about by our biological conditioning, we don't have any idea what freedom really means.

Remember the Buddha's words: "All that we are is the result of what we have thought." If our thinking is based on stimulus and response, he is trying to tell us, then most of us live like puppets, moved by patterns of thinking built up over years of repetition. These habits of mind cause us to say and do certain things habitually. They motivate our actions and mouth our words, and we just go along.

When we lose our temper, for example, it is as if anger were a puppet master, sticking two fingers up into our head and stimulating all the old control centers to make us move. "Start fussing and fuming *now!* You know how. Remember?" When we act on these angry impulses, we are adding to our habitual angry response. After a time, we have precious little choice in how we respond to the frustrations and irritations of everyday life. Someone gets in our way and we can't help exploding. It is not as if we choose to get angry. Anger — what yoga psychology calls the anger samskara — is making our decisions for us.

The same mechanism is at work in all our rigid, conditioned emotional reactions — resentment, jealousy, lust, anxiety, greed, self-will, and their hundred and one relations. We would be amazed if we could look below the surface level of consciousness and see how many of our problems are caused by these deep-seated habits of thinking. This is a distressing sight, but it serves a vital purpose: it fires the desire to rise once and for all above the tyranny of our mind.

How can we do this? Is it possible not to be batted back and forth between spiritual and physical demands?

Yes, the mystics answer with one voice, it *is* possible. We can learn to make every response a matter of free choice. If we can ally all our personal efforts with the upward drive of evolution, it will carry us beyond the reach of physical conditioning to a state where love, resourcefulness, and vitality are spontaneous and free.

"In the river of life," says another ancient yoga text, "two currents flow in opposite directions. One, on the surface, flows toward sorrow, toward sickness, toward bondage. The other, beneath it, flows toward happiness, health, and freedom."

This may be fantastic hydrodynamics, but it illustrates our predicament perfectly. If we stay at the surface and do nothing, this image suggests, life will still take us somewhere — but not where we want to go. Staying in one place is not an option. To catch the deep current that leads to freedom, we have to swim and swim hard, against the flow of every conditioned response.

Again, the Buddha's words give us the key: "All that we are is the result of what we have thought." How does the mind become conditioned? By thinking the same thoughts over and over and over. To get free, then, we have only to think opposite thoughts over and over. That is why the Buddha called his way of life *patisotagami:* "swimming against the current" of selfish living, in order to merge at last in the flow of love that is our real nature.

This is not just for the thrill of mastery. The Buddha is not the kind of teacher to tell us to do something contrary simply because it is hard, or to do something painful simply because we learn from pain. Going against the current has a very down-to-earth purpose: the reconditioning of the nervous system, so that we can rise above the dictates of pleasure and pain.

In all of us, the nervous system is conditioned to strict one-way traffic: toward what we like and away from what we do not like. Any attempt to drive against this traffic brings a cry of protest from body and mind. This reaction is only natural; it is part of our biological inheritance. But pleasure and pain are part of life. Often we find it necessary to do something unpleasant or forgo something pleasant for the sake of a higher goal. At such times we need the full cooperation of our body and mind, a nervous system that can face life's challenges without complaint. This is not merely spiritual living. It is the essence of a stress-proof personality, which everyone in the modern world needs.

"Yoga," says the Bhagavad Gita, "is evenness of mind." When you can keep your mind on an even keel in good fortune and bad, in pleasure and pain, when you can be kind to those who like you and to those who do not, then you have reached the state of yoga: you are free.

Between senses and sense objects, the Gita explains — for example, between the taste buds and a fresh pizza — there is an intimate affinity which has nothing to do with us. Our dog Ganesha has a similar affinity with buttered toast. The moment he senses a piece he has to have it, even if he has already eaten. And then he can't just gobble it down. He has to go over to a particular spot, next to a particular yellow dandelion, and fold his paws around his toast in a particularly dainty way; only then can he eat. That is just what the senses do with sense objects, the Gita suggests, and there is no need for us to jump in. I enjoy watching Ganesha enjoy his toast, but I don't get emotionally involved. If there is no toast for me, I don't get depressed or feel deprived. His job is to eat; mine is to watch and enjoy.

Similarly, the Gita says, although sensory events have a compelling effect on the body and the mind, they really have nothing to do with us. We think we are involved because we identify ourselves with the body. Our real Self, pure spirit, is the detached observer, who watches life with quiet compassion, always free to enjoy.

In the Bhagavad Gita, the Lord tells his disciple Arjuna:

> "When the senses encounter sense-objects, a person experiences cold or heat, pleasure or pain. These sensations are fleeting; they come and go. Bear them patiently, Arjuna."

This is profound, practical philosophy, with a touch of humor in it too. "Arjuna," Lord Krishna asks teasingly, "When you have your bath, do you cry if the water is warmer than you like? Do you get angry if it is a little too cold?" Temperature is just the contact of water with skin, sometimes pleasant, sometimes unpleasant. On a cold morning it is enjoyable to have a hot shower; after a hot day, it is refreshing to plunge into a cool river. Everybody finds these experiences pleasant. But we don't spend a lot of time thinking about them. We don't go around telling everyone in the office, "I had a hot shower this morning!" or go to bed depressed because the bathwater was too cold. It is the same with the mind. Just as we experience a momentary sensation of warmth or cold on the skin, we feel a momentary sensation of liking or disliking in the mind, as fleeting and insubstantial as a shadow.

Our usual response, however, is to cling to things we like as if they could last forever — and without realizing it, we cling to things we dislike too. When someone says something objectionable we comment to ourselves, "I don't like that person." And we keep on saying it, despite all the other things he or she may say or do; we can't let go. "This is just a momentary touch of unpleasantness," Sri Krishna would say. "Why get excited over it? Don't give it any more attention than you would a tepid bath."

Of course, this is difficult to do. But even more difficult is to look on pleasure in the same way. Sri Krishna's advice here is thoroughly original. When he says, "Put up with pain," Arjuna nods; he is a warrior and can understand that. But when Krishna adds, "Put up with pleasure too," Arjuna rubs his ears. "That's right," Krishna says. "Bear it patiently. It comes and goes. Don't run after it, and don't try to cling to it when it comes your way." Pleasure is as fleeting as suffering. In fact, as the Buddha says, most of our suffering comes from trying to cling to pleasure, trying to build happiness on a sensation that comes and goes.

The artistry of this appeals to me deeply. Today, after more than twenty-five years of taking Sri Krishna's words to heart, if you see me in a pleasant situation and ask, "How are you doing?" I will say, "I'm bearing up." I am enjoying myself, but I am patiently keeping my mind unruffled too — in fact, it is only a calm mind that can really enjoy. Then, when something unpleasant comes — as it is sure to — I can say, "I'm bearing this well also." If it does not sound paradoxical, I enjoy life when fortune is against me just as I do when fortune shines.

When you apply this, you see Sri Krishna's mischievous sense of humor. After a date at a gourmet restaurant, if your boyfriend or girlfriend asks, "Did you enjoy yourself?" just say nonchalantly, "Oh, all that pleasure! I think I stood it rather well."

With this kind of detachment, pleasure leaves no residue of compulsion in the mind — no emotion-charged memory, no craving to look forward to the next time. Ordinarily, after a satisfying sensory experience, the mind immediately wants to know, "When can we do that again?" The memory sits in the mind like a time bomb, waiting for a suitable opportunity to explode into behavior again. There is very little freedom in this, which greatly curtails our capacity to enjoy. Even to enjoy a sensory experience, we have to be detached. Remember those lines of William Blake:

He who binds to himself a joy
Doth the winged life destroy;
But he who kisses the joy as it flies
Lives in Eternity's sunrise.

વ

Years ago, when my wife and I were looking at old houses, we came across a once-gracious garden with an ancient marble fountain so clogged with rubbish that not a drop of water could get through. You don't just give up such a fountain for lost. With a lot of cleaning, you can get the water to start playing again. Then grass and flowers will grow around it, and birds will come there to have their bath; it will grace the garden with its beauty.

It is the same with personality. To remake ourselves, we don't have to bring goodness, love, fearlessness, and the like and stuff them all in somehow. They are already present in us, deep in our consciousness; that is why we can never really rest content with being anything less. If we work to remove the impediments that have built up over many years of biological conditioning, to dislodge all the old resentments and fears and selfish desires, love will flow from us like a fountain, and those we live and work with will come to us to be refreshed.

Here the spiritual figures of other times can give us confidence by their example. Ask Saint Augustine if his behavior as a young man gave any hint of the treasures of the spirit hidden inside. He would laugh. "Ask my parents," he would say. "Ask around my home town. They will tell you what a sigh of relief they breathed when I left for Carthage, burning with my desires. 'You weren't the same person then,' they say — and in a sense that is true. That young man was a pauper, insolvent, worth nothing much, a burden on most everybody. In his place today there stands a prince, bearing gifts for all."

And if we ask, "Is this a miracle, then?" Augustine would just smile. "Not at all. It is the result of a tremendous amount of loving labor. I had to teach my mind new ways of thinking. But the hardships are not over-whelming if you want more than anything else to bring your destiny into your own hands."

Of all that is wonderful in the human being, our most glorious asset is this capacity to change ourselves. Nothing is more significant. I admire the achievements of science, but I do not feel intimidated by the current conviction that we are what our genes are. My body is what my genes make it, but my character and behavior are not fixed by my genetic code. As proof we have the lives of great men and women of all religions who have thrown these claims to the winds with their personal transformations — from angry to compassionate, from insecure to unshakable, from human to divine. The message of their lives echoes down the corridors of time to those who have ears to hear: "You are not what your body is. Your real nature is spirit, which nothing can diminish or deny." Whatever our past, whatever our present, all of us have the capacity to change ourselves completely through the practice of meditation.

PART 3

Strategies for Freedom

Obstacles and Opportunities

EVEN AFTER ALMOST thirty years of teaching meditation, I still am amazed at how much more there is to say about it. Words simply cannot communicate some of the marvelous experiences which it is our birthright as human beings to look forward to as contemplation deepens. Until you yourself get into the submarine that is meditation and enter the dark waters of the mind, far below the glittering surface of consciousness, there is no way to fathom these experiences. But even those who meditate sincerely and systematically face serious obstacles which must be overcome before they can penetrate the recesses of this vast, uncharted ocean that is the mind.

The Buddha enumerates five such obstacles: sensuality, ill will, laziness, restlessness, and anxiety or fear. Each of these locks us out of deeper consciousness. Like an inner tube around a swimmer's waist, they keep us from diving below the surface of the mind by entangling us in the thoughts and experiences of the outside world.

Let us look at these obstacles one by one.

1. Sensuality

"Sensuality," in the Buddha's language, is not a term of moral judgment. It refers simply to our human tendency to become entangled in the impressions of our senses — to become so attached to what brings sensory pleasure or pain that we lose real freedom of choice. This is a normal biological response, but when we are trying to enter and master the world within, it keeps us oriented in just the wrong direction. To turn inward, we have to detach ourselves from the hold the senses have on the mind; there is no other way.

Unfortunately, our whole civilization seems involved in a conspiracy to stimulate the senses more and more. Every day, in the newspapers and magazines I look through, the films I see (or walk out on), I am amazed to what degree this tendency is exploited. Look at the pages of even those prestigious magazines which cater to educated, sophisticated men and women. Every ad is aimed at this singularly low level. The so-called New Wave advertising is expressly designed to stimulate our senses to an extreme degree. I would call it Old Wave, simply less subtle than before.

The Buddha gave us a useful rule of thumb for dealing with the senses: neither asceticism nor overindulgence. Don't do everything your senses tell you, he would say, but don't try to starve them into submission either. Train them to be your friends and allies. That is what the Buddha called the Middle Path, the road to health and happiness for everybody.

When I try to apply this today, I usually begin with the compulsive urge to eat when it is not necessary. When you are hungry, eat what is best for your body. Eating at any other time shows very slight regard for health, and the mind becomes obese and tyrannical when it gets its way like this at the expense of our better judgment.

Simply put, in the matter of food, following the Middle Path means taking a healthy interest in food but not making food the end of life. I enjoy good food when it is time to eat, but until mealtime comes I don't think about food at all.

Advertisers, by contrast, seem to want us to think about eating twenty-four hours a day. Whenever I go to the supermarket, I notice how the covers of many popular magazines display endless varieties of sweets. Under their influence it is very easy to get into the habit of bringing home this little treat and that little tidbit to munch on. Even if you don't have an eating problem, this habit of automatic buying and snacking takes a real toll on the mind. It weakens the will, divides attention, and keeps thoughts turned outward toward the sense-world — just the opposite of what we need to enter the world within.

If you love your children, I would say, don't get them into the "sweets" habit at all — and if you love adults, don't encourage them in it. On a special occasion, I do sometimes treat my teenage friends to a gooey chocolate confection. They can take it. But it's not a special occasion every time we can find a convenient excuse. If every event is celebrated with chocolate or candy, a lot of calories are going to find a home around somebody's waist.

If I may say so, as spiritual teachers go, I am really very lenient in these matters. The important thing is to remain clear about your goal; then it is easy to keep a reasonable perspective.

Like many Indians, for example, I still enjoy tea — in fact, friends have given me a special blend that was a favorite of Prince Charles and Princess Diana. You may compliment me on my good taste. I enjoy my midafternoon cup of "the beverage that cheers but does not inebriate." On the other hand, the moment I find my mind looking forward to tea-time or taking it for granted, I change my routine, which keeps my mind on its toes. I am concerned about caffeine, but my first concern is the mind. Too much tea can injure the nervous system, but anger does much more harm. If you give up anger, you can even drink coffee now and then. These are all matters of common sense.

For most people, this same artistry can be applied with alcohol. When I go to a wedding I toast the bride and groom with champagne, but on other occasions I simply decline. You may find this awkward at first, but you will be guarding your mind against getting caught in a sensation, which can happen so gradually that you may not even notice. Nobody has ever been offended when I said "No, thank you" at a party where drinks were being served. I don't think anybody ever thought I was a wet blanket. Almost everybody respected my position — partly, I think, because I passed no judgment on others.

I have had many friends who were victims of alcohol but freed themselves from its power through the practice of meditation. One of them paid me a great compliment: "You're a good sport. You never hit below the belt." I know how hard these habits are to give up; I know that the further they progress, the less power we have to choose. But even the most tenacious, long-standing addiction can be conquered. No matter how deep it has gone, with patient effort in meditation we can always go deeper and uproot it from underneath.

With any addiction, the bonding is very much like a kind of cement my friend Stuart once showed me — Krazy Glue. If you get a drop of Krazy Glue on your fingers and accidentally touch your eyelid, you may need minor surgery to get your fingers free. The mind is like that. It has a tremendous capacity to get attached to anything on earth; it is making Krazy Glue twenty-four hours a day. "Get it while it's fresh," the mind says brightly. "Take as much as you like. The more you take, the bigger the discount." That is the mind for you. Whether it is an addiction to food or drink or smoking or any other physical indulgence, the dynamics of this bonding are always the same.

Here you can see the enormous practicality of the Buddha's presentation. You don't have to treat each addiction by itself, he says. Simply remember to respect the cementing capacity of the mind, and just as you wouldn't touch Krazy Glue to your eyelids, don't touch these potent sensations to your mind. These are not just moral issues for me, any more than they were for the Buddha. His Middle Path is based purely on a clear understanding of how senses and mind function.

Being a good spiritual scientist, the Buddha divides sensations into three convenient categories for us: pleasant, unpleasant, and neutral. This is not a fixed classification. Sensations can change places; that is where we have freedom. What is pleasant the first time may be unpleasant the fifth; and, most liberating of all, we can take an unpleasant sensation which is in the interest of others and move it joyfully into the "pleasant" category.

The first few times you indulge your senses in a particular way, the Buddha would explain, there is only a sensation. It has no emotive force behind it. But when you start thinking about pleasant sensations over and over, craving to have them again, then the process the Buddha calls *asava* begins. The word shows his sense of poetry as well as his precision. *Asava* actually means an intoxicant, distilled from fruits, flowers, or trees. When a sensation is fresh and new, the Buddha implies, you look at the pretty bottle it comes in and read, "Only two percent alcohol by volume." In other words, you are only thinking about it once in a while; the alcohol content is low. So you say, "What does it matter? Two percent isn't going to do me any harm. I can still function." But the fermentation has begun; that is the danger. The craving is brewing. Whatever the sensation, whether it is food or drugs or sex, the process is the same.

As long as there is no craving involved, there is no bonding between senses and sense-objects. As long as there is no craving, you won't go and raid the liquor cabinet of that sensation against your will. But once fermentation has brought the alcohol content of the sensation to fifty percent, that craving has come to stay. You can't help thinking about it; it can't help thinking about itself. Then it can no longer be classified honestly as a sensation; it is an obsession.

Any liking or slight attachment is a potential obsession. As long as it remains minor, one can enjoy it. If you like coffee or tea, make it a minor attachment — take it or leave it. The same goes for healthy entertainment of all varieties. But if it is smoking, do not even flirt with danger; leave it. And if it is alcohol or potent mind-bending drugs, take your money and run.

At this juncture, it may help to venture for a moment into the Buddhist theory of cognition. (I promise the tour will be brief!) In the act of seeing, the Buddha would say, there are three separate elements: the eyes, the object, and an act of attention. When all three come together, there is sensation. Right now, for example, I am seated at a beautiful desk given to me by friends. While I am looking at the desk, I can appreciate its beauty. But when I am reading at it, I do not really see it; my attention is completely absorbed in my book.

The application of this abstract idea is highly practical: if you can withdraw your attention, no sensation on earth can have any hold over you. That sensation simply will not be there for you; it will have no connection with your mind.

When attention is under this kind of control, all the senses are your friends. If they wander off into areas where they can get into trouble, you have only to call them back and they will obey. This is what you have been doing in meditation all along, bringing your attention back whenever it strays. Now you can apply the same skill during the day, whenever the mind feels attracted by some old sensory habit.

Without this kind of control, however, the habit itself compels attention. Then you have no choice: if you see something you desire, your mind will not stop thinking about it until it is good and ready. When we have a strong liking or disliking for something, we cannot really see that thing for what it is. A fog comes between us and that object, a fog of potential obsession. Our attention is not really on the thing in question; it is locked onto our liking or disliking.

The next development in sensory obsession is anger. You try to go on satisfying your desires, trying to get what you want either in some relationship or some possession or experience, and things keep getting in your way. That is life. But the more this happens, the further the fermentation process goes. The desire becomes obsessive. You get frustrated, irritated, resentful, hostile, angry — which means that the alcohol content of the craving is enough to put you under the table.

I once asked a friend just how much alcohol a drink can have. "Well," he said, "there's a brand of Puerto Rican rum called '151.'" I was impressed. Rum that is one hundred and fifty-one proof is seventy-five percent alcohol. This is a good description of anger: you are drunk and can't get inside your own consciousness to see what is wrong. On rare occasions, just like someone drunk on alcohol, you get sentimental, but most of the time you are increasingly difficult to get along with. That is how one develops an "angry personality," a condition that is almost an epidemic today.

When this happens you are continuously angry, constantly hostile — if not overtly, then beneath the surface, where thoughts simmer unaware. You see things that are not there and act on situations that simply do not exist the way you perceive them. It is impossible to reason with people in this advanced condition; they are drunk with anger. And the primary cause is getting involved in sense-stimulations to the point of obsession. Anger is the final development of the Buddha's first obstacle.

2. Ill Will

The second obstacle, ill will, is perhaps the most serious impediment in meditation. According to the Buddha, ill will expresses itself in one hundred and thirty-five forms! Each of us has a regular catalog of them. That is what makes ill will so difficult to recognize at first, leave aside how difficult it is to tackle. If only we could get a catalog of negative mental formations like the ones that come in the mail every other week from L. L. Bean! Fortunately, says the Buddha, tackling ill will does not require becoming familiar with the whole catalog. What we have to do is learn how to undo the underlying habit of mind — again, the asava.

Sensations in the mind ferment just the way sensory impressions do. When somebody ignores our predilections or fails to do things our way, we get an unpleasant feeling which is familiar to everyone. At first it may last no longer than writing on water. But when this feeling comes frequently, it starts fermenting. Now, just as with a sensory experience, we don't have to feel dislike every time life crosses us; we can simply withdraw our attention. But when our attention is riveted on ourselves, every negative experience adds to the alcohol content of our ill will. The diagnosis is penetrating. We develop a tendency to dislike — not just to dislike this or that but simply to dislike, period. Whoever comes in the way of that dislike gets it.

The Buddha uses strong language here, to shake us out of

our bad habits. You are not being very bright when you dislike someone, he says. Don't blame that person; he or she has merely happened to come in your way. Your disliking asava is *inside,* fermenting away; that is all that is happening.

On thousands of coconut palms in my native state of Kerala you will find pots hanging to collect the sweet milk of the trees for brewing toddy. The Buddha must have been familiar with a similar sight in the villages of northern India. As the liquid sits in these pots, it ferments and becomes so strong that crows who drink it sometimes start cawing at midnight. "It's not time to get up," my grandmother used to explain when we heard this. "The crows are just drunk." This is the attitude behind the Buddha's compassion. The fellow who flies into a tearing rage is not responsible, he says. He is "under the influence." Don't hold it against him; he can't see straight. That is what ill will does.

Let us take a closer look at this fascinating distilling process in the mind. Take the case of a resentment — over what your boyfriend said to you last weekend at that fancy restaurant, for example; or, more accurately, over what you thought he was saying. While the resentment is fermenting, you are busy thinking to yourself over and over, "Oh, so *that's* what he meant!" Then you start rehearsing things to say to him when you run into him again.

At times like this, what we are really doing is slowly developing a compulsive tendency to think in negative terms. In fact, we are working on that tendency very hard. The issue is not what that particular person said or did not say, meant or did not mean. The real issue is that we are developing a tendency to dwell compulsively on what *anybody* says to us — which means we are developing a tendency to get upset. We are making ourselves upsettable, emotionally fragile under stress. After enough of this fermenting, our mind will boil at the most harmless little thing. We will be at the mercy of everyone. The Buddha's final diagnosis: we do not generally suffer from others; we suffer from ourselves.

The cure is to go against that habit. Never accuse others or blame them; try to refrain even in your own thoughts.

When the liquor of ill will is ready to flow out of the bottle on the slightest provocation, put the cork back in the bottle and push it down hard with your mantram. After all, there is always going to be a certain amount of unwitting unkindness in life. It is up to us not to become unkind in turn.

A six-year-old friend of mine once provided me with a good illustration of this. He likes dates but does not think much of figs. A few mornings ago, in the hurry of the moment, I gave him a fig I had saved for him from my breakfast. When I realized my mistake, I was a little anxious about what he was going to say. He was wearing his usual very thoughtful expression. It touched me when he turned to his mother and explained, "I don't think Uncle meant to give me this." Cultivating a positive attitude, you see. It was true: I forgot he is a date man, which I should have remembered. His courtesy is a lesson from which all of us can learn.

When somebody is curt to us, it is easy to take it personally. But this is a habit which can be unlearned in the same way it was acquired. Pull back from your mind a little and remind yourself, "Why get angry? The poor fellow may not have slept well. Maybe he hurried through his breakfast and tripped on the stairs; he's probably still getting over all these indignities. Why should I hold it against him?"

Today I don't even have to work at this response. It has become second nature to do everything I can to cork up a fermenting asava. My mind no longer goes into turmoil; it is always at peace. But I had to learn this the hard way, just as everyone does: by trying to do it over and over and over, even when it hurt.

In secular psychology the problems of resentment against parents are dealt with in one class; then you go and deal with the problems of competition between partners in another. The mind-catalog has so many varieties of asava that you will never have time to take classes for them all. By focusing on the asava process, however, we can see that essentially there is only one kind of ill will. A resentful person from Topeka will have much the same asavas as a resentful person from Taiwan. The way to protect yourself against any ill-

will asava is the same: do not let your mind dwell on any unpleasant memory or negative thought. This precious capacity comes as meditation deepens.

When somebody has gone on a drinking binge, my
friends tell me, the first thing to do is "dry him out." This is
just what the Buddha recommends for an asava too. If you
were to go to the Compassionate Buddha and complain,
"That person makes me so upset!" he would reply drily,
"You're not being quite accurate. You don't get upset because he makes you upset; you get upset because your mind
is upsettable. Why don't you make yourself less upsettable?"
Use the power you draw from meditation to change the al-
coholic asava of ill will back into the milk of kindness — not
by breaking off your relationships, but by being with people
even if they upset you.

This may be hard on you, but if it is any consolation, it is
probably hard on them too. Work with them, support them,
refrain from unkind remarks and unkind acts. That is the
way to develop good will. I am not blind to selfish motives,
but I never avoid people. I refuse to allow resentment to
cloud my eyes or lessen my love. I can be firm with people;
there are occasions when I have to be stern. But I don't think
anybody misunderstands this sternness as lack of love.

I want you to know that I was not born with these capacities. This kind of patience and endurance came only after a
lot of practice, working with people who could be quite
difficult. All of us have the same capacity for maintaining
harmonious relationships. What we need to develop is the
will to bear with people when the going gets rough — to
stick it out, as you say. And that simply comes with trying.

Here we can see why the Buddha has been called such a
supreme psychologist. Those who like to be separate, he
says, make a practice of disliking people because the more
they dislike, the more separate they become. The opposite,
fortunately, is just as true: the more you practice liking
people, the more deeply you will feel one with them — and,
miraculously, the deeper you will find yourself going in
meditation too.

This strategy of doing the opposite of what a compulsion

dictates is also the answer to a tragic state of mind I sometimes run into, where someone will tell me in all honesty, "I just don't like myself." This is one of the worst possible kinds of ill will, largely because it undercuts one's capacity to change. If we look on it as the same asava of ill will, however, the treatment becomes simple. When you are always kind to others, kindness becomes an attitude. Your natural response is to be kind. Then you cannot help being kind to yourself as well; you will develop a habit of supporting yourself.

The splendor of the human being — every human being — is our capacity to learn from past mistakes. I never ask anyone, "Why did you make that mistake?" I ask only, "Have you learned from it?" This was always Granny's emphasis when I was growing up. The Buddha, similarly, is trying gently to warn us about life's method of teaching us the adverse effects of ill will. "If you do not learn from the harm your ill will causes others," he tells us point-blank, "life will find ways of hurting you more and more."

This is where the Buddha uses a term which I translate gently as "slow on the uptake." The Buddha doesn't expect us to be saints; he just asks that we use our heads. Our problems are of our own making, he says, and the way out of our problems lies in making wiser choices in how we think and act toward others. This is actually a very hopeful approach, which never dooms any human being as "wicked" or "lost." It is only when we refuse to learn from our own mistakes that we find we are leading ourselves into despair.

3. Laziness

This third obstacle is easy enough to understand. Just as laziness is our enemy in making money or in gaining prestige or power, it is our enemy in spiritual growth. Hard work is absolutely necessary for excellence in any field, and nothing requires more intense effort than meditation.

This may sound odd, because intense activity is generally motivated toward goals that are just the opposite of spiritual. But over the years I have made a rather surprising observation: the person who is relaxed, easygoing, "laid back," may not be a good candidate for meditation. Such people simply may not be willing to put forth the effort required to make difficult changes in personality, or have the energy and the stamina to keep going when the going gets rough. To go far in meditation, we need to rouse all the energy we can muster and then channel it all toward one overriding goal.

One of my favorite illustrations of this is the story of James J. Lynn, a prosperous American businessman who had spent immense amounts of time and energy in drilling for oil. Lynn was attracted to an Indian spiritual teacher named Yogananda Paramahamsa, who came to this country early in this century to found the Self-Realization Fellowship. Yogananda told him, "You have a lot of energy, but you are wasting it just drilling for oil and making money. Why don't you drill into your own consciousness and really strike it rich?" Lynn did, and the energy and self-discipline that had made him an oil tycoon took him a long, long way in meditation.

But it is not enough to be full of energy. Many people have plenty of energy and don't know what to do with it or how to focus it, so they scatter themselves over a hundred and one fascinating projects that do no one any good. We need to be able to gather all our capacity for energetic action and then harness it to the goals of spiritual living.

To do this, we have to learn to be detached from the results of our work. Detachment brings confidence and clarity of vision. When obstacles arise, if you are detached you won't lose your nerve; you know you can turn obstacles into opportunities. And when opposition comes, you can face it squarely and learn from it without stress or agitation. Detachment means withdrawing your personal energy from secondary activities; discrimination is seeing where to focus that energy, so that all your choices take you closer to your goal.

I must say in appreciation of this country that laziness is not a national weakness. Daring and ingenuity are qualities you seem to possess in abundance. If all this energy and enterprise can be harnessed in spiritual living, I have no doubt that our next generation will grow up in a much better world. When it comes to setting social trends, to inventing whole technologies, to setting world records, the people of this country have no equal.

What amazes me even more, however, is the kind of thing Americans do in their spare time: scaling the Transamerica Pyramid in San Francisco, riding a pedal-powered glider across the Atlantic, skydiving, or ferreting out a way to tap into the computer system of a big university. You have two weeks of vacation and you can't think of anything interesting to do, so you break the code of the university's computer. The human being needs goals worthy of this kind of enterprise and daring; otherwise, at best, they are wasted. I am thinking primarily of young people, for I think they feel this lack of a worthy goal even more keenly than those of us who are older. It is my fervent hope that gradually we can introduce to them goals worthy of a whole lifetime of daring pursuit.

4. Restlessness

The fourth obstacle, then, is restlessness. It can take many forms, but essentially restlessness simply reflects the fact that the mind cannot bear to be still. Some people do not like to do a job the same way twice; they have to keep coming up with variations. Others cannot live without something to worry about. All of us know people who have to talk. And when restlessness invades the body, we always have to be up and doing something, going somewhere — what and where do not much matter; the important thing is to keep moving.

Of course, this can invade meditation too. I still have people coming to me with a particular complaint: "After fifteen minutes of meditation I just can't sit still." There are all kinds of things to try when this happens, depending on the person. "Before you meditate," I suggest, "go for a fast walk repeating your mantram. If you're really restless, go for a short run." But the mind is not easily conquered. "I tried that," one fellow told me, "but after I run, I'm so relaxed I fall asleep." Trying to corner me both ways.

Restlessness can mean different things. Often it signals the rise of energy that is crying out to be harnessed, which is a very promising sign. The person who can't find a challenge big enough, who roams the globe seeking new places or thrills and can't manage to settle down to a humdrum job, may be just ripe for meditation: looking for something that can't be found in the external world, ready to turn inward.

Once you start meditating, restlessness is the same signal, but now it means the time has come to go deeper. When we hit a pocket of resistance in consciousness, a samskara that is difficult to face, the mind has two common ploys: either it gets restless and turns to all kinds of irrelevant distractions in the outside world, or it gets lazy and falls asleep. In either case, the strategy during the day is the same: hard, selfless, concentrated work, preferably for the benefit of others.

As long as we recognize it and harness it, restlessness is a positive sign. Restlessness is energy being released, which is bound to happen as meditation deepens. But all this energy has to be harnessed; otherwise it will drive us into irrelevant activities that at best keep us from going deeper, and at worst may get us into a lot of trouble. That is why hard, selfless work is an essential part of spiritual living.

When you feel a restless mood coming on, therefore, treat it as a hopeful sign. But be sure that you stay in the driver's seat. Don't let your mind take the wheel and drive away. This energy comes as a precious resource to enable you to deepen your meditation, expand your circle of compassion, and make a greater contribution to the welfare of others. Deeper reserves of energy are a trust; they are not meant for self-aggrandizement. My advice is to find something useful which helps other people and then throw yourself into it wholeheartedly.

Some people work eleven and a half months just to be able to sun themselves on Copacabana Beach in Rio for the other two weeks of the year. But while they are lying on the sands of Copa, the mind can't get out of overdrive: it is back in the office, or worrying about some domestic problem, or— most fascinatingly — off on its own vacation in some other time and place, daydreaming some fantasy or reminiscing about the azure waters of the Greek isles. This is the fatal flaw in restlessness: the mind always has to be some-where else. The secret of joy lies in being one hundred per-cent where you are all the time, which means the mind has to learn to be still.

Almost every day I go for a walk on the beach, and every time it is new and fresh. When somebody says, "You must get tired of that same old beach!" I say, "On the contrary. Every day it is a new beach for me. I see it with new eyes." When nothing ever palls, nothing ever gets stale, nothing is taken for granted, then everything becomes a miracle — a miracle full of unending joy.

5. Fear

The last obstacle is fear. Actually, the word the Buddha uses is a general term that includes all kinds of apprehensive possi-bilities: not just being outright fearful that something might happen to you or your family, but also feeling uneasy inside, uncomfortable about the future, vaguely worried, more than a little afraid.

One particularly common form this obstacle takes is anxiety — that vague sense of feeling apprehensive, you know not of what; the nebulous, lurking fear that you are unequal to life, unable to cope, sinking under some unseen pressure. Such sensations have become so pervasive that our times have been characterized as the Age of Anxiety.

As we reflect on this, we find that as usual the Buddha is talking directly to us all. Each of us is granted a certain mar-gin for committing mistakes in life, particularly in our younger years. A certain resilience is built into our physical and mental apparatus. But we cannot expect to go on com-mitting the same mistakes over and over and not suffer for them in time. Anxiety, in this sense, is often a helpful re-minder of where we stand on the self-graded scorecard in-side. It signals a kind of learning problem that can be easily solved once it is understood.

Anxiety, the Buddha would say, stems essentially from not being able to be what we want to be — which, in turn, comes from not knowing who we really are. These mis-apprehensions can go deep into consciousness; so please do not be impatient with yourself and expect anxiety to vanish overnight. Yet nothing dispels anxiety more effectively than meditation, because it goes straight to the heart of the problem: not on the surface, but deep within the mind. When you are meditating sincerely and systematically, every day brings you a little closer to your real Self, a little more at home in a world you can deal with. Even if there is a big gap between who you are and what you want to become, you have the tools in your hands and know how to use them. It brings hope, confidence, and the growing sense that you are equal to whatever the day may bring.

There is another secret too, one I have already mentioned. When fears and anxieties stem from low self-esteem, part of the problem is this almost universal samskara of judging. As we learn not to pass judgment on others, we cease to apply harsh standards to ourselves. Forgiving others, liking others, is a swift, sure route to forgiving and liking oneself.

Meditation and its allied disciplines — training our senses and passions, training attention, putting the welfare of others first — are learning tools. "Don't pine over your mistakes," the Compassionate One is reproaching us gently. "That will only make you more insecure and anxious." Learn from your mistakes and draw on them to deepen your meditation. Learn from them and enrich your life.

"More than anything," the Buddha would continue, "I want you to be free of these five obstacles. I want your physical, emotional, and spiritual health to improve, your life to be always fresh, your relationships always rich, your contribution always valued. And I want you to have the good opinion of the person whose approval is most difficult to win: yourself." Then we can say, as the Buddha did toward the end of his life, "I am the happiest of mortals. No one is happier than I."

Strategies for Freedom

IT IS IN THE MIND that the Buddha's five obstacles arise, and it is essentially in the mind that we must tackle them. The problem is that the mind is an extremely subtle thing — in fact, it is not a thing at all. You cannot go to the store and buy a *Complete Mind Repair Made Easy* manual, full of advanced circuitry diagrams and step-by-step instructions. The mind is a dynamic, ceaseless process, full of twists and turns, of intangibles and imponderables.

Yet, intangible as it is, the mind-process *can* be studied from within. More important, we can learn to change the channels through which its energies flow, which leads to the transformation of character and consciousness.

These are simply engineering skills. With the aid of meditation, I have ventured to explore every murky turn of the vast field of mental currents that we all have inside. Now, when someone comes to me with a problem, I know exactly how to put my finger on the source. Through the practice of meditation I can help that person find the leaks where vitality is being lost, rechannel a wandering flow of attention, harness the power of a compulsive attachment, unblock the flow of love when the waters have run almost dry.

It is in terms of the dynamics of these mental skills that I want to present what might be called the Buddha's five strategies for freedom. Simply by observing his own mind with detachment, he has hit upon techniques which people like you and me can employ successfully to follow in his footsteps.

❧

The first strategy is literally "changing one thought for another": a negative thought for a positive one, an unkind thought for a kind one. "Just as a carpenter uses a small peg to drive out a bigger one," the Buddha says, "you can use a right thought to drive out one that is wrong."

When I recommend a particular set of inspirational passages for meditation, this is the purpose behind my advice. An appropriate passage for meditation has certain requirements. It should be positive and life-affirming, and it should return you to the world feeling confident and equal to its challenges. I have compiled a small anthology for meditation, *God Makes the Rivers to Flow,* with precisely these requirements in view. It is a selection of positive passages which you can use effectively to drive negative thoughts out of your mind.

The Prayer of Saint Francis of Assisi, which I always recommend for meditation, makes a perfect example. When used sincerely and systematically, it can replace the most deep-seated of negative attitudes with inspiring, lofty ideals.

This strategy can be applied effectively throughout the day as well. We need to do this frequently, in fact, to counteract the influence of all the negative thoughts we have already driven in by thinking them over and over, with lots of help from the media. There is an art to this. With practice, as your concentration deepens, you can drive in the positive peg without any danger of smashing your thumb.

To give one small illustration, whenever somebody is unkind to me, I can immediately unroll the panorama of that person's good qualities. Instantly the balance is set right. As with most skills, this is a matter of practice. When you are having trouble getting along with someone, a simple first step is to sit down quietly and recall how many times that person has given you support. You are using positive memories to drive out negative ones before they have a chance to crowd together and form a mob, which is all resentment really is.

Often you can do the same thing with a physical craving. Imagine, for example, that you are minding your own business when up pops a craving for something chocolate. Most of us, I trust, have experienced this. It's not anything abnormal. But you cannot afford to go on eating chocolate every time you get the urge. Even if your waistline can afford it, you are trying to train your mind.

This may be a good time to bring out a smaller peg: take a handful of raisins and start eating them instead of the chocolate, repeating your mantram all the while. If your craving for chocolate is really strong, give yourself the raisins one by one. Chances are that your palate will eventually give up and sigh, "Leave me alone. I don't want any more raisins, and you can forget the chocolate too."

When it comes to sex, on the other hand, I would never recommend this approach. Trying to dislodge a strong sexual desire with a little indulgence, the Hindu scriptures say, is like trying to put out a fire by pouring butter on it — or, if you want to make the image more modern, by pouring on gasoline.

Of course, sex has a beautiful place in a completely loving, completely loyal relationship, where it expresses the deep desire to be united on a much more than physical level. But even in a loving, loyal relationship a disproportionate amount of our capacity to desire often flows into this channel, consuming our vitality. That is what makes harnessing sexual desire — not repressing it, harnessing it — one of the most practical issues in all of daily living.

What makes these impulses difficult to deal with is the fact that we keep on thinking about them. This gives them enormous power. And as if we couldn't supply our fantasies with enough material on our own, the media swamp us with images and messages designed to associate sexual satisfaction with the most unlikely services and products. Why, for instance, a car is supposed to appeal to us in this way I have never been able to understand.

When you have a strong craving that is difficult to cope with, therefore, don't spend long periods of time analyzing it, thinking it over, dwelling on it, brooding over it. Throw yourself into hard, selfless work, especially in the company of other people; you will find that a good deal of the power in that craving will be transformed as you work at deepening your relationships and your meditation.

This is an extremely important connection. I have been talking in terms of spiritual engineering, which, like physical engineering, often comes down to energy. Sexual desire is power — one particular expression of the power we use to think, to work, to live, to will, to love. And power is neither good nor bad. It can be used for creation or for destruction. It is the same with the energy of creative desire.

We need new words in this connection, and Sanskrit provides a very accurate term: *kundalini*. Kundalini is an intensely concentrated form of vital energy. It is the power behind love and the fuel for spiritual progress. When this power is released through the transformation of sexual desire, you can use it to build loving relationships everywhere. The power is the same; whether it is used physically or spiritually is a matter of direction. As you begin to realize that you are a spiritual being instead of a physical creature, you find you are drawing on this power to love all of life. Then you do everything possible to let this love flow through practical, beneficial channels.

This is the key to the puzzle of sex. When somebody tells me, "I keep thinking about this all the time," I have a positive answer. "You're generating a lot of energy," I say. "You've got power to burn. But all that has to be used." Otherwise, at best, it is wasted, which can have far-reaching negative implications for your health.

Those who have a number of close, personal relationships, based on tenderness and respect rather than on sex, have a perfect context for harnessing and transforming the power in sexual desire. If they pour this power into deepening their relationships, they will find that the sex urge seldom becomes oppressive and that their vitality seems unending. This is not suppressing sex or denying it but simply gaining a say in how and when it is used.

There is nothing wrong in having strong sexual urges. This is our vital capital; this is where our power lies, locked up. When we channel this power, it nourishes all our relationships. Eventually it becomes a fountain of love that flows continuously into our daily life. But most important, kundalini has an evolutionary purpose: it is the immense store of energy we draw on for the transformation of human consciousness, the fuel for the long, difficult journey to Self-realization.

I want to repeat that this is not in any way a plea for stifling the sexual faculty. It is a method for putting to work a faculty so huge that it can never be fulfilled on the physical level. Once kundalini is roused and channeled, you have a deep reservoir of tenderness that brings the capacity to touch people deeply and kindle their love and tenderness in turn, even to the point of disarming their hostilities.

This is a terribly important issue today. It is because we spend our energies so unwisely that most of us feel inadequate to do anything about the violence and alienation taking place in our communities before our eyes. Translated into global proportions, this profligate waste of time and energy on petty, personal pursuits amounts to a general lack of love for our fellow human beings. Its impact on world events today is staggering. When you are working to transform your faculties and unify your love, you can feel equal to any challenge, no matter how difficult or threatening it has become. That is our real capacity: endless.

❧

The next strategy is reflection. When you are being propelled by a fierce craving, the Buddha says, stop and reflect on the consequences of giving in.

At such a time, of course, most of us cannot even think of sitting down to think things over. Our mind is racing, and all we want to do is jump in and act. Before trying to apply this strategy, the first thing to do is slow your mind down; only then will you be able to think clearly. Repeat your mantram until the pressure to act on the craving has abated. A fast walk repeating the mantram helps greatly, but if you cannot get out, try writing the mantram a set number of times — say, one hundred — slowly, neatly, and with concentration. As your mind grows calmer, you can make it reflect on past experience — all the consequences of similar mistakes that made you tell yourself, "Never again!"

Repeating the mantram sounds mechanical, but its effect is profound. You are actually using the power of a compulsive craving to send the mantram, with its calming influence, deep into your mind. That very act strengthens your will, increasing your ability to withdraw your attention from what you crave. Every time you do this, the mantram goes deeper; the next time, it will reach deeper still.

When you feel a strong craving to demolish a big stack of pancakes, dripping with fresh butter and maple syrup, consequences may be the furthest thing from your mind. There is nothing wrong with pancakes if you can stand the calories, but if we go on yielding time after time, we develop a habit of yielding — not just to pancakes but to anything. Any impulse, including anger, gains increasing power to claim us. "Remind yourself of these problems now," the Buddha says. "Reflect on them, and then start strengthening your capacity to say no. It will serve you well in every activity of life."

What the Buddha is asking us to cultivate is reflective thinking. I distinguish this from "reflexive thinking," a phrase from Norman Cousins which aptly describes what happens in our minds when we are being driven by an urge. The Buddha is a teacher who respects our capacity to reason and reflect. Gradually, as we develop this capacity, we should be able to consider the consequences not only of actions but of mental states like anger. We should be able to see how anger spreads and grows until it gains the power to disrupt any relationship anytime it chooses.

Then, once we understand these connections, we should start putting the Buddha's suggestions into practice. When we find ourselves in a situation in which insensitiveness or anger is urging us to ride roughshod over other people's feelings, we should summon the detachment to go for a fast walk around the block or through the woods or up and down the hall, silently repeating our mantram the whole way. Once our mind has quieted down, we can reflect with some detachment on how painful the long-term consequences of our anger are likely to be for everyone, including ourselves.

It may help also to understand the positive consequences of not yielding to a negative emotion. The ancient Hindu sages say that our normal span of life is one hundred and twenty years. This is a magnificent concept. According to them, to die at age sixty or seventy is to fall victim to a premature death. By this accounting, which does not contradict some of the current biological theories of aging, we all have potential for health and longevity far beyond what we use. Negative emotions like anger can devastate the body. By not yielding to such emotions, we can dramatically increase our chances for a long, healthy, active, happy, worthwhile life.

ॐ

The Buddha's third strategy is withdrawing attention. When distractions come in meditation, paying attention to them only strengthens them. That is the time to give more attention to the inspirational passage. We can use the same strategy during the day as well. Many personal problems involve distracted attention — the mind getting caught in an unproductive or negative track. When we learn to withdraw our attention from such problems, we begin to see that even in meditation most distractions have their source in what we do and think during the day.

You can see how rare undistracted attention is today.

Everywhere we are conditioned to be distracted. When I go to a movie theater, I can't help noticing what great difficulty children and young people have in keeping their attention on a film. First they have a short conversation during the opening scenes. Then after ten minutes they get up, return with a big carton of popcorn, and proceed to give at least half their attention to that. Eventually the mind learns to be fractioned like this all the time; then learning problems are inevitable.

Much of the blame for this can be traced to the methods of advertisers. Distraction is the basis of their trade. Madison Avenue agencies have long conferences to figure out what distractions we will fall for most readily. Subliminal advertising, which they have raised to a polished skill, is designed expressly to slip distractions into our minds when we are not even aware, so that we will slip money out of our pockets with equal lack of awareness. Combine this with a television habit—Americans report that their households watch TV an average of seven hours a day — and you find that the mind is conditioned to be divided and distracted several times an hour every day.

If you practice pulling your attention away from distractions, even minor ones, during the day, you will find distractions much easier to ignore in meditation. The habit of working with steady concentration will reward you with new depth in meditation and a mind that is unflappable in times of stress or challenge. And if you can curb the propensity to get upset or jealous or uncooperative, which is the mind getting caught in emotional distractions, you will find major stumbling blocks beginning to melt away, both in meditation and in your personal life.

"If thine eye be single," Jesus said, "thy whole body shall be full of light." In everyday language, when we are able to keep our attention undistracted, everything shines with wonder. Even from my own small experience I can testify to what a marvelous extent this is true. I have cultivated the habit of one-pointed attention for decades now, and today I could not divide my attention even if I tried. When your attention is complete like this, as the Christian

mystic Angela of Foligno says, "the world is full of God."
Everything shines with divinity and beauty, part of an indivisible whole.

Walt Whitman is trying to express a similar idea, I think,
in *Leaves of Grass:*

> To me every hour of the light and dark is a miracle,
> Every cubic inch of space is a miracle.
> Every square yard of the surface of the earth
> Is spread with the same. . . .
> What strange miracles are these!
> Everywhere.

Many years ago I had a number of beatniks among my
friends. When I used the word "miracles," they would say
skeptically, "Tell us about one." Every moment you remain alive is a miracle. Talk to medical people; they will
tell you there are a million and one things that can go
wrong with this body of ours at any given instant. It is
only because we have not developed the capacity for appre-
ciating miracles that we don't see them all around us. Life
is a continuous miracle: not only joy but sorrow too; not
only birth but death too. That is what undistracted attention allows you to see everywhere.

But the most important miracle of all, as the Bhagavad
Gita says, comes in the climax of meditation: "You will see
the divinity in every creature." In the long run, this is what
focusing our attention on the bright qualities in people will
reveal. Once the mind learns to be completely one-
pointed, it is ready for the ecstatic moment when it merges
utterly with the object of its devotion. At first this happens
only for a blissful instant in meditation — as one Catholic
mystic says, just for the span of one *Ave Maria.* But that is
enough for us to see with the whole of our being that the
divinity in our hearts is our real Self, and that that shining
Self is the same in all. Then being kind and loving no
longer requires effort; it is our native state. In traditional
language this is the vision of God, which the great scriptures and mystics assure us we can live in continuously if
we allow no other purpose to come in our way.

ஃ

It is only fair to warn you that the Buddha is slowly backing us into a corner. This is his method of drawing his audience deeper. Often he starts out talking about familiar topics which do not challenge us much, but slowly he brings his scrutiny closer and closer until we find him right in front of us, looking us straight in the eye. Now he is upon us, saying, "The fourth strategy is 'Go to the root.' The first three strategies are preliminary. Now it is time to remove the real cause of your problems: why you get jealous, why you find yourself in a bad mood so often, why you get resentful with so little provocation."

This is not to say that the first three strategies are unimportant. Without them we cannot even speak of going to the root of personal problems; they go so deep in the mind that we cannot reach them. But when our meditation can penetrate like a microscope, the Buddha can show us the bacillus that has been causing all our personal problems: self-will.

Some of the bacilli studied in medical school, I understand, can hide behind a number of symptoms. Self-will, similarly, is the root cause of problems very disparate in appearance. Some are so familiar that we think they are normal, or at worst beyond our control. Jealousy is one particularly strong form the infection takes. In a competitive society jealousy has to be rife, because comparing oneself with others is the very basis of both. Jealousy may disguise itself as mild and rational — over a friend's appearance, a co-worker's success, a neighbor's new car, a brother-in-law's happiness or prestige. But jealousy in any form is malignant. If it becomes a habit of mind, it can erode our security and self-confidence to a fragile shell.

There is no reason to be surprised if we find ourselves afflicted with this condition. We are conditioned on all sides to compare ourselves with others, to climb higher by pulling others down, to gain by taking, to win by making others lose. The few times I have gone to sports events in this country, for example, I have been pained by the language coaches sometimes use to spur their teams. By the end of the third quarter, the simple "Go get 'em!" has been replaced by the even more primitive "Kill!"

The antidote to this kind of overzealous competition was given by an English poet in familiar lines: what matters is "not that you won or lost — but how you played the game." Often I don't even remember who wins a good match. I remember a spectacular match between Bjorn Borg and Jimmy Connors when I was so full of admiration for the play on both sides that at the end I exclaimed, "Why don't they give a first-place trophy to both players?" The preoccupation with winning is not at all a mature outlook to cultivate. No matter how high the stakes, as human beings we should manage to keep our opponent's welfare in view as well as our own. This attitude will help us stay free from the severe anxieties and animosities that overzealous competition breeds.

The quality we *should* try to cultivate is the exact opposite of competition. The term in Sanskrit is *mridu:* soft, gentle, tender, sweet. In the *Mahabharata,* the tremendous epic of which the Bhagavad Gita is a small part, a beautiful verse reminds us that one who is really strong is gentle. Only a weak person resorts to harsh, rude, vengeful behavior. Those who are full of inner strength can tire you out with their patience, their consideration, and their unflinching love.

In a personal relationship, I don't think anything can be more effective. Coming from a large matriarchal family, I grew up in an atmosphere where women practiced this kind of strength as a way of life. I can proudly say that I have yet to see anyone who did not respond to tenderness in action. Even when momentarily angry or agitated, everyone responds to the kind of tenderness that is tough inside, that can oppose when necessary without being brusque. Without this kind of inner toughness, the Buddha tells us plainly, it is not possible to maintain a continuously loving relationship with anyone.

To find successful representations of love these days, either in art or in life, is like coming upon an oasis in a desert. The Buddha gives us far higher standards. We should learn to be continuously in love, he implies; and not only that, our love should always grow. We should never allow ourselves to fall out of love; otherwise love cannot last.

From this you can get some idea of the immensity of the task he is laying out for us. Yet it is possible for all of us to aim for what Catholic mystics call "love without an object," in which anyone who comes within our orbit receives the fullness of our love. This is the lofty state that the sincere practice of meditation and its allied disciplines can put within our reach.

The moment somebody says, "I don't like that person," I tell myself, "What an opportunity!" I am not being rhetorical. That is how I see a dislike now: as a grand avenue opening up onto a more joyful future. "She irritates me" translates as "She can teach me to be more patient." "He intimidates me" can be heard as "He gives me the opportunity to make myself unshakable." Again, this is a matter of emphasizing the positive everywhere. Every ordeal we can look on as an opportunity to become stronger and more patient; every confrontation, as a chance to learn how to cooperate. Every obstacle in life can become a precious opportunity to grow.

This is why the Buddha calls his path "going against the current." If you want to follow me to freedom, he says, be prepared to swim upstream, against the river of conditioning. Be prepared to grapple continuously with the fierce flow of your negative mental currents. Struggling like this builds up our muscles. In time our strokes will become almost effortless and our sense of purpose irresistible.

When you feel jealous of somebody, therefore, the answer is not in competing; that will only make your case of insecurity worse. Why should you compare yourself with anyone? The very basis of security for every one of us is the assurance that the Lord dwells within us as our very Self. The deeper you go in meditation, the more sure of this you feel, the more at home with yourself and the world around you. Whoever you are, whatever your weaknesses, you know you can fulfill the purpose of your life and be a blessing to many others.

Every one of us can make an enormous contribution to life. What is important is how steadfastly we are practicing the spiritual disciplines that bring us closer to life's goal. When you are giving this effort your very best, nothing that another person has, nothing that another person is, can draw your envy. Gradually you will come to feel that you live in everybody. What reason could you have to envy anyone on the face of the earth?

❧

The Buddha has been building toward a tremendous climax. With the first strategy he starts out tickling us with a feather, as it were. Then he coaxes us along with a branch. Finally, when he is sure we can stand it, he cracks us over the head with the whole trunk. That is the Buddha's way, and he is going to bring on the trunk right now. "After you have learned to deal with the mind in these four ways," he says, "prepare yourself for *abhinigraha.*" It sounds ominous, and it is. *Nigraha* means "destroy"; *abhi,* "completely." "Kill the very source of your difficulties," the Buddha says, "and then make doubly sure that it is dead." That is the Buddha for you.

After you have been meditating sincerely for years, you will find that a number of beneficial changes have gradually been taking place. You have learned how to deal effectively with most difficulties in life, and the quality of your daily living has improved immensely. But you have descended gradually to a level of consciousness where your compulsions, your asavas or samskaras, are few but ferocious. Instead of a hundred Lilliputians to fight with, you now face a mighty Goliath. You may not recognize him at first, but you feel there is something very familiar about him. Small wonder: he is the ego, your very own expression of separateness, selfishness, and self-will.

At this level we begin to see clearly how many of our

difficulties in life, particularly in personal relationships, have been caused by this arrogant creature. Fortunately, by this time we have also developed enough compassion not to blame ourselves, any more than we blame other people for their shortcomings. Otherwise we could easily be overwhelmed by a sense of guilt. We are making an amazing discovery: this petty creature is not who we really are. He is an imposter, pretending to be us, and all these years he has fooled not only others but ourselves. This discovery frees us to put all our energy into fighting back against the ego without quarter.

In the Christian tradition this aggressive figure is called the devil. There is practical wisdom in this tradition, for it reminds us to identify not with the ego but with the Self. The Sufi mystic Jalaluddin Rumi answered those who said they did not believe in the devil with a simple statement: "Look into your own hearts." The devil merely personifies the dark forces that every human being has inside: self-will, violence, anger, greed, jealousy, revenge.

The struggle with self-will goes on and on and on, throughout the day and eventually throughout the night. Actually, this is a struggle that we take up from the very first day of meditation, and the harder we try at the disciplines, the sooner we will win. This is the culmination of all our years of struggling at spiritual growth. We are in the finals, at Wimbledon on Centre Court. Do Steffi Graf or Jimmy Connors complain when they face a rugged opponent in the finals? They find a fierce joy in it; they know the very difficulty of the challenge will draw out their best. The Buddha's words of encouragement are in this same vein: "Clench your teeth." That is a literal translation. Play hard, he says, and every time you lose a point, hit back — by defying a selfish urge.

You will come to find a wonderful exhilaration in this battle. The rounds can go on for hours at a time. They can be drawn out for days, weeks, even months together, with a lot of give-and-take on both sides. You get worn out, but you hang on out of sheer determination.

Yet there comes a time in the lives of even great mystics

when they lament, "I cannot do this by myself. How can I defeat my own self-will?" This critical juncture is when the spiritual teacher comes to the rescue. My own teacher, my grandmother, taught me from a very early age to defy my self-will. Much later, after I took to meditation, she was able to awaken in me the overwhelming desire not to be dictated to by self-will under any circumstances. This great desire gradually began to draw the power of all my other, smaller desires; finally, all my desires flowed together into the colossal desire to defeat self-will and be free. That is why it is so important to strive to unify desires from the outset. Ultimately there is not the slightest doubt that everyone who practices these disciplines with sustained enthusiasm can and will win this battle. The main question is how long we are going to let ourselves get knocked about first.

The central asava in self-will, remember, is the tendency to get selfishly attached. Earlier I used the word "obsession." Most people have an inherent tendency to dwell on things, to think about something over and over and over. We developed this precious capacity through millions of years of evolution. I say "precious" because one-pointed absorption, when free, is the secret of genius. Without it, we could never learn to meditate. But usually this capacity is not free. That is what happens when we dwell on ourselves. Then thinking becomes compulsive and we lose the choice of what to dwell on. It is this adhesive asava of attachment which gets us stuck in all sorts of difficulties, particularly in personal relationships.

To paint a vivid picture of this elusive character, Self-will, and his typical habits, I am going to draw on a pastime which I usually don't even like to mention: fishing. The seriousness of this topic calls for a strong image. So picture, if you will, Self-will as the Father Asava, seated on his riverbank in one of those fold-up hammock chairs and decked out in waterproof rubber pants, fishing in the troubled waters of consciousness. He has his cooler full of beer close at hand in case he gets bored, but usually you will find him about to nod off, with a slightly wicked grin on his face, waiting for an unpleasant memory to happen along. When he feels a nibble on the line, he jerks into action and slowly starts reeling it in, involving us more and more in a negative line of thinking.

What happens when we become the victim of an obsession is easy to picture. Even if we have been caught before, the bait seems so attractive that we still feel we have to bite. We may even come to believe that being caught by Father Asava, that dangling at the end of the line with a hook in our mouth, is the greatest thing in the world. If we are not careful, Father Asava will reel us in and stick us away in his little basket.

You can imagine the determination and courage it takes to keep swimming in the other direction while this fisherman is slowly reeling us in. It hurts to pull loose from an asava, especially if the hook has gone deep. That is the kind of effort required to undo a powerful asava like resentment.

Much more efficient, of course, is not to get hooked in the first place. Yet even when an obsession is fairly strong, there are still ways to take out the hook. One is to refuse to act on that obsession, however strong the pull. You may not yet be able to change your line of thinking, but you can make a good effort not to speak or act the way it is urging you to; otherwise you are playing into the fisherman's hands.

A second way is to not incriminate other people. Those who fall into the habit of blaming others for their compulsive attachments and obsessions are swimming straight for the hook and biting hard. When you feel that somebody is causing you trouble, for example, or purposely trying to agitate you, or pursuing you, or avoiding you, remind yourself, "This is just old Father Asava, fishing in troubled waters." You may find it helpful to keep a little reminder on your desk or calendar, where you can see it often. It will help you, and it will help the people you feel inclined to blame as well.

Here is the positive side: this same capacity for habitual obsession, if we can win it over, becomes a splendid capacity for continual contemplation. That is the intent behind each of the eight points in my program. I think it is also the reason that the Compassionate Buddha never advocated ascetic practices but always taught the Middle Path. Virtually all our human faculties — our senses, our emotions, our imagination, our intellect, our will — are meant to serve us as friends. We should win them over, not crush them, because we are going to need all of them as our allies later on in the struggle against self-will.

In practical terms, what does it mean never to be hooked by self-will? It means the agitation in your mind ceases. Everybody, I think, knows the feeling of helplessness that comes with an agonizing memory, a paralyzing fear, a maddening conflict. We just don't know what to do, and the memory, the fear, the conflict, repeats itself over and over and over in our mind. The agony lies not in the memory or fear or conflict but in the repetition. When we are not hooked by self-will, we can stop the repetitive agitation of the mind cold. When the mind is still, how can there be agitation? We still grieve when others suffer, but we do not suffer for ourselves; and our grief for others releases the will and resources to love and help and serve.

The key to this is detachment — detachment from our own ego, which is terribly difficult to cultivate. Here, devotion to a divine incarnation — Jesus, Sri Krishna, the Buddha, the Divine Mother — helps greatly, for it gives us a focus for our love outside the narrow compass of self-will. The subtlety is that this divine focus is not outside us. The Lord is our real Self, embodying the divine qualities which all of us have within us.

It follows that when we are looking for the Lord, unifying our desires to realize him, the Lord is looking for us at the same time. Meister Eckhart, the towering mystic of medieval Germany, goes even further: the eye with which you see God, he says, is the same eye with which God is looking all the time at you. Imagine peeking through a keyhole in the mind and seeing the Lord looking back at you! We don't realize that he can open the door to deeper consciousness from inside; yet silently, subtly, all the time we are banging away on the door, he is undoing the latch on the other side. This is what devotion to a spiritual ideal can do.

My own spiritual ideal is Sri Krishna, whose teachings in the Bhagavad Gita give us a perfect manual for spiritual living. The literal meaning of the name *Krishna* is "he who attracts us" — he who draws us to him, right from within. The pull the Lord can exert is infinite, yet he can only draw us as close as we want to come. Only when we throw aside our excess luggage, the dead weight of our love for self-centered pursuits, can he draw us to himself.

I have learned to look upon Sri Krishna as my divine employer, my Boss. He takes much better care of us than we do of ourselves. From the first day I saw how he cares for those who serve him, my heart has belonged to him. There have been instances in the early days of the Blue Mountain Center when, being human, I sometimes made poor decisions. But such is Sri Krishna's love that he says, "Even though your decision was wrong, the consequences are going to be right because you were trying to act in my service." This is infinite love. After all, what boss on earth will say, "You've made a poor decision, but I'm still going to promote you"?

This is the assurance you get when you devote your life selflessly to a supreme cause. Even before Self-realization, if you have done your best and still find yourself getting caught by an asava or sinking under the steady attack of self-will, the Lord will guard you if you call on him sincerely with all your heart.

When you realize the divine Self within you, the Bhagavad Gita says, you are launched beyond superficial living like a missile. Your joy and your capacity to contribute to life are multiplied a million times. To inspire us, the Buddha has given us in one sentence a model of ourselves as glorious and yet as human as any we could ever desire. "Love the whole world," he says, "as a mother loves her only child." Love like this will plunge us into deepest consciousness and release in us the power to make a lasting contribution to all of life.

PART 4

Inner Space

CHAPTER II
Voyagers

TWO HUNDRED YEARS have passed since the first successful passenger balloon was launched, when scientists discovered it was certain death to venture more than five or six miles above the earth's surface: there was very little life-supporting oxygen beyond that level. Everyone concluded that five or six miles was the farthest possible extent of human reach beyond the surface of this earth. Speculation about worlds beyond our own would have to remain in the realm of science fiction.

Similarly, most people today still would not accept the idea that there are whole worlds within our consciousness, each as real as the world outside us. Even those who accept a kind of inner reality find it fantastic to talk about exploring realms which are, by definition, beyond our conscious reach.

Today, of course, travel in outer space is a reality. I doubt that we have begun to guess at its problems and dangers, but even schoolchildren now know that there are ways of circumventing this scarcity of oxygen and the myriad other difficulties of getting to the moon and back alive. Yet inner space remains a mystery; it can scarcely even be conceived. Even the most brilliant thinkers balk at the paradox of taking the light of consciousness into the depths of the unconscious and coming back whole to tell the tale.

Professor Huston Smith, whose little classic *The World's*

Religions I heartily recommend, calls India the world's introspective psychologist. If you look in the Upanishads, the oldest known statement of the Perennial Philosophy in the world, you will find some daring speculation into the nature of the universe and the human being's place in it. My submission is that this is hardly speculation. These ancient sages actually found ways of entering into the subconscious, traveling there at will, and coming back to let us know what they had discovered. Not only that, their methods have been passed down from generation to generation in an unbroken tradition that goes back perhaps five thousand years or more.

I was fascinated to read that the real beginning of space travel came late in the nineteenth century, when a deaf schoolmaster in a little Russian town about one hundred miles south of Moscow hit upon the idea that a rocket was the answer to the problem of how to travel safely far into space. It was not merely a question of power; he had come up with a way to extend a little piece of our earthly environment into realms where life as we know it cannot go. In the same way these mighty Indian sages, wanting to plumb the far reaches of the universe within, hit upon the idea that in order to understand the core of Reality, one has to go deep, deep into one's own consciousness.

This was a dazzling discovery, breathtaking in its implications, as we shall see. Just as a rocket will lift you high into the infinity of outer space, meditation will plunge you deep into the infinity of inner space. And just as today we have courageous astronauts, in those days India had what we might call "Atmanauts" — after the Atman, the divine Self, which they discovered in the reaches of deeper consciousness.

The more I read of modern astronomy and cosmology, the more I stand amazed at how these sages, with no billion-dollar Inner Space Program for support, were able to arrive at discoveries which advances in science are only now beginning to corroborate. Great sages like Katha, author of the Katha Upanishad, established ashrams on the slopes of the Himalayas and along the banks of beautiful rivers like the

Ganges. There they lived with a few daring students, training them to undertake this stupendous journey into the unconscious. Because this journey was so dangerous, so undreamt-of, they needed the daily support and guidance of someone who had already discovered a route to the Self.

From experiments in the laboratory of the mind, these ancient sages discovered that the entire created universe proceeds from and is sustained by the Infinite. That is the literal meaning of *Vishnu,* a word Hindus use for God to this day. As if this weren't enough, these sages have also given the world what Huston Smith calls the most daring hypothesis in the history of mankind. By turning the laser of complete concentration to illumine the vast realms of the unconscious, they found that the Infinity which is the source of creation is within you and me.

In the Upanishads we find glorious poetry describing, as far as words ever can describe, this very personal discovery. Sage Katha, speaking through Yama, the King of Death, says: "In the depths of consciousness the Lord of Love is ever enshrined" — in everyone, everywhere, all the time. "No sun shines there, neither moon nor stars, nor flash of lightning, nor fire lit on earth." No external light of any kind is needed there, for our real personality is all light, all love, always shining. As Saint Teresa of Avila testifies, it is day without night, a world of perpetual light. Even the sun and stars borrow light from the light of consciousness. "The Self shining, everything shines after him." This is the glory of the human being.

It is almost too great a revelation to absorb. Yet when I look at the sun now, I remember the penetrating words my spiritual teacher spoke to me many years ago: "One day that sun will burn out, but *you* will never die." I thought then that this was a grandmother's loving hyperbole. Today, on the strength of my own small experience, I can assure you that you too will never die — as you can discover for yourself if you embark on this great inner voyage.

The great mystics of all religions testify unanimously that when you discover this divine core of your personality — call it Christ, call it the Buddha, call it Krishna, call it the

Divine Mother, call it simply the Infinite — you are not just transformed; you are transfigured. You are no longer in love merely with persons A, B, and C; you become love itself. You *love;* therefore you love every person on the face of the earth, irrespective of country, race, culture, caste, or sex. And from then on it is not possible for you to think ill of anybody or to hurt anybody, because you have discovered that your nature is love. You work to live your life in a manner that never infringes on the happiness of anyone. And as far as possible, you try to contribute to solving the immense problems that face humanity.

As Sri Krishna says in the Bhagavad Gita, such a person lives in love. No matter what the circumstances, whether among friends or among foes, he dwells in the City of Love always. The Sufi mystics put it beautifully: "My Beloved, whom the great galaxies cannot contain, is contained in my little heart." This is the inexpressible miracle of Self-realization.

To such a person the rest of creation testifies, "He lives in me too." This brings a sense of being at home everywhere in the universe, which is the very basis of ecology. Saint Francis spoke of Brother Sun and Sister Moon; you and I may speak of Mother Earth: all of us are part of an indivisible family.

Wernher von Braun, the scientist who laid some of the cornerstones of space exploration, says simply, "There is beauty in space, and it is orderly." He is reporting to us about a world of which we know very little. Similarly, I can report from my own small experience that the unconscious is exquisitely beautiful, the very source of beauty. And it is orderly; it can be traveled. My own travel in the unconscious has been systematically, carefully planned. We can all go there and come back, bringing with us a wealth of understanding which we can use for enriching life.

Von Braun goes on to say: "If you know the laws of space and obey them, space will treat you kindly." If you know the laws of spiritual living, the unconscious too will welcome you with open arms and treat you kindly. It is in this difficult, dangerous search for the Infinite, under the loving guidance of an experienced teacher, that we human beings grow to our full height, reach out with our hands and touch the stars. Yet at the same time we stand firmly on Mother Earth, able to be of service to everyone who comes in contact with us.

This goal, I assure you, is within the reach of every human being. I used to complain to my grandmother, "This calls for superhuman capacities, Granny, which I simply don't have. You're doing me a great disservice by thinking I can do what cannot be done." Her answer went straight to the point: "You don't know what your capacities really are." None of us knows, none of us can know, until we discover them by reaching beyond ourselves.

Just as those celebrated divers at the southern tip of India are able to plunge deep into the sea and come up with pearls, you and I can learn to dive deep into the fathomless depths of consciousness until we too come up with a "pearl of great price," the worth of which the universe itself cannot match. That is the kind of resources we have lying within us, waiting to be drawn up into everyday life. The Buddha refers to these resources in the mantram *Om mani padme hum,* the "jewel in the heart." When we discover this jewel, through years of patient effort, our whole personality begins to shine.

In India, spanning a period of more than five thousand years, we have an unbroken string of little people like me — very ordinary, committing most of the mistakes that ordinary human beings everywhere commit—who have been caught, to use Meister Eckhart's picturesque phrase, by the Divine Fisherman, the Lord or Self within. I like to imagine Sri Krishna seated in the unconscious under a shady tree with his pole and line, holding his flute casually against his lips and playing a haunting melody, waiting for someone to take his eyes off the feverish pursuit of selfish satisfactions long enough to notice him there. Suddenly he feels a sharp pull, and who should turn up with Sri Krishna's sweet hook in his mouth — and a sheepish look on his face — but some very ordinary fellow like me.

When this happens to us, our first thought is, "Why

should this happen to me? There are millions of more deserving people in the world; why doesn't the Lord catch them instead?" Sometimes, as Eckhart says, we thrash about, trying to escape. But the more we struggle, the deeper the hook enters. After that, nothing but Infinity will satisfy the infinite hunger in our hearts.

There is a great deal of travail, sometimes a heavy load of suffering, involved in coming to grips with this infinite destiny. The challenges of traversing the world within are almost more than a human being can bear. When at last we discover in ourselves the divine source from which the universe comes, we echo what mystics in every religion have exclaimed: "How could I, so limited, so human, ever have attained this sublime discovery except through the loving help of a power beyond my own?"

Whether we refer to a transcendent Self or to the touch of some personal form of God, this experience of grace is the very basis of devotion: the boundless love that Saint Teresa of Avila felt for Jesus, or that Sri Ramakrishna felt for the Divine Mother. Either way, we realize then that this help from within far transcends the petty limits of our individual, everyday personality.

Yet grace does not just come along and carry us to our goal — not even if we are saints. A great deal of effort is required.

Here I often recall a five-thousand-year-old tale. In my native state of Kerala summer is followed by the monsoon season, when the sky reverberates with the roll of thunder. According to the Upanishads, the thunder is trying to tell us something: *Da-da-da!* The first *da* means *datta:* give; do not grab. The second stands for *damyata:* be self-restrained, be self-controlled. And the third, *dayadhvam,* reminds us, "Be kind": kind to all, whatever is done to you. That is the lesson of the thunder.

When I hear a thunderstorm today, however, I hear another message as well, taught and practiced by spiritual seekers down the ages. The first of my "three *D*s" is determination, the will to succeed against any odds. The second is detachment: not a cold withdrawal from life, but detachment from one's own ego. And third comes discrimination, the capacity to see life's goal clearly and keep it in focus always.

These "three *D*s" are my own lesson from the thunder. We can think of them as a three-stage booster for the exploration of inner space. Let me elaborate on them one by one, for they speak directly to the needs of our own times.

CHAPTER 12

Determination

TERESA DE CEPEDA Y AHUMADA, later to become loved around the world as Saint Teresa of Jesus,
grew up as a beautiful, high-spirited girl from one of the
most distinguished families in the sixteenth-century
Spanish town of Avila. With charm, intelligence, keen artistic sensibilities, and a saving dose of common sense, she
seemed to have the world at her feet. Yet while still in her
teens, this passionate young woman had already begun to
find the attractions of worldly life too small to satisfy her.
She felt their pull — would be torn in two by it, in fact, for
more than twenty years. But nothing could silence a much
deeper appeal within her, a call to a far higher destiny.

Some dim awareness of an infinite promise deep within
her must have prompted her to turn inward. In her writings, Teresa describes candidly what was taking place inside. "All the things of God gave me great pleasure," she
recalls, "but I was held captive by the things of this
world." Yet the inward pull would not let her go:

> Reason tells the soul how mistaken it is in thinking that all
> these earthly things are of the slightest value by comparison
> with what it is seeking. A little recollection reminds it that all
> these things come to an end. And faith instructs it in what
> the soul must do to find satisfaction. . . .

Young Teresa had seen what life offers on the surface,

and it was not enough. She longed for much greater challenges, deeper awareness, something more lasting than this world of change. "There is no joy in the finite," the Upanishads say. "There is joy only in the Infinite." Teresa's soul yearned for the Infinite, and nothing less would satisfy her.

Teresa of Avila is so appealing a figure, so human and yet so inspiring, that we naturally want to know her secret. How can we be like her? What enabled her to turn herself inward heart and soul? Is it something that lesser figures like you and me can follow?

As it happens, Teresa did leave us her "secret." In her autobiography, she stresses over and over the one quality she found vital: *determinación,* determination, decision, will. "Those who have this determination," she declares, "have nothing to fear."

Determination? Is that all? Surely, we think, some loftier, finer qualities must come before this mundane one. But then we reflect on our own experience. In any walk of life— arts, sciences, sports, entertainment — wherever excellence is achieved, there is one quality we almost always find: the sheer will to overreach oneself, to keep going whatever the odds until the goal is attained. Saint Teresa is simply reminding us that we need this same quality to reach an infinite goal. The same determination with which we pursue passing, personal satisfactions can be used for spiritual growth.

If we find that we are not making the kind of progress we would like on the spiritual path, Teresa is suggesting, the reason may be simply that we are not trying our hardest. We may have all kinds of other reasons, but often the problem is simple lack of determination.

I often notice delivery trucks with a sign on the back: "Frequent Stops." One I used to see regularly in Berkeley was Danny's Diner, which stopped so frequently that it never got more than a block from campus. This can happen in meditation too. There are people who meditate for a few days and then stop to experiment with some old indulgence. When they take up meditation again, their mind is even more rebellious and they fall asleep. So they stop once more. Their mind and senses are offering resistance, meditation is no fun, so they say, "Why not go in for a few healthy distractions?" This approach will take us no farther than Danny's.

"Many have begun," Teresa observes, "but never persevere to the end. . . . What His Majesty wants is our acts of will." In Sanskrit we have a word which means "heroes at the beginning": people who take up a job with a fanfare of trumpets but soon find that their enthusiasm has tiptoed down the back stair. Those who go far in meditation are the ones who keep on plugging. They may not be very spectacular; they may never hear a trumpet. But they keep on trying day in and day out, giving their best in every situation and relationship, never giving up. Such people are bound to reach their goal.

ॐ

The first challenge to determination, of course, comes up every day. "Shall I meditate today at my regular time and place, for the full length of time? Or shall I fudge a little?" So many things can come in the way!

This one little question is so common, so insidious, that I want to stress just how important it is. Nothing you can do will strengthen your determination more than the regular practice of meditation: at the same time, and for the full length of time, every single day.

No one finds this easy or convenient. Everybody faces obstacles: you are traveling, you have a cold, your baby starts crying, you get interrupted by a phone call, you have to wait for a call that never comes . . . The list goes on forever. Some obstacles, I agree, cannot be removed until you change your job circumstances. But most can be dealt with through surprisingly simple measures which never occur to us — unplugging the phone, for example, or getting up early enough to let the baby sleep. Just by meditating regularly, you are deepening your determination immeasurably.

On the other hand, if you neglect your meditation, you

can be sure that your mind will take full advantage of it on the following morning. In the Indian spiritual tradition the saying goes, "If you miss one morning's meditation, it takes seven mornings to make it up." If you miss seven mornings — well, you can figure it out on your computer.

One of the first things I learned about training the mind was to put meditation first always, whatever obstacles or temptations come in the way. When I came to this country, almost thirty years ago, I was on a ship for nearly a full month. The Peninsular and Oriental steamship company apparently never felt motivated to provide meditation facilities, and the cabin I shared with other Fulbright scholars would not serve. Among other things, the only fresh air it ever got was supplied by a little tube not much bigger than my thumb.

One of my friends saw the expression on my face and asked what was wrong. I tried to explain, as best I could, about needing to get my full quota of meditation morning and evening. He brightened helpfully. "See here, old boy," he said, "you've been in harness such a long time now. Why not take advantage of the circumstances and enjoy a well-earned vacation? Everybody enjoys a holiday, and here you are getting one free. Why keep talking about meditation? You can do all that when we get to America, where you will need it."

"I want to be on vacation always," I objected. "That's just why I never miss my meditation."

The next morning I got up very early and went exploring. Soon I discovered the sports deck, absolutely deserted in the early hours of the morning. I wrapped my blanket around my shoulders, sat down, and closed my eyes, and once I began going through the second chapter of the Bhagavad Gita I forgot all about where I was. When I finally opened my eyes, I found I had been amusing a small crowd of bystanders. I let them laugh; after all, there is not much to do on board a ship, and I didn't mind having a reputation for being a colorful character. People laughed, but gradually they came to respect me. "He's a really earnest chap," they would say, "whatever that Indian thing is that he's doing."

That was not the end, either. The tests went on. Eventually our ship reached Port Said, on the Suez Canal. Egypt was not only the land of the pharaohs to me. For hundreds of years it had been a great center of Islamic civilization, and President Nasser had attracted interest throughout the newly-independent states of the Third World. The Fulbright commission did not share our enthusiasm about Nasser, but it had made extensive arrangements to take us scholars to Cairo, several hours' journey across the Sinai peninsula, and to house us there and show us around.

This news was greeted with great joy. My friends, knowing how keen I was on seeing Cairo at last, brought me the itinerary as soon as it was announced.

"It will be wonderful," I agreed when I saw the schedule. "But I won't be able to come with you."

They were shocked.

"Not come with us? Don't you want to see the Nile, the Pyramids, the mosques, the bazaar? Haven't you been telling us about Al-Azhar University, almost a thousand years old?"

I said simply, "You know how much I want to see them."

"You may never get a chance again."

"I expect I won't. Certainly not as the guest of the government."

"Well, then?"

"If I follow that schedule," I explained, "I won't be able to maintain my meditation." And that, they knew, was that. I never have seen Cairo. But I have seen the Self.

So be regular in your meditation, be systematic in following the instructions, and try to sustain your enthusiasm no matter how you feel. Every morning when you sit down for meditation, renew your determination. If you believe in a personal God, ask for the help of Sri Krishna or Jesus or the Divine Mother to make this decision unbreakable. If you do not believe in a personal God, ask for help from your own deeper Self, the Atman. Either way, it is important to remember that you are appealing to a power deep within you, not to anyone outside.

Meditation, of course, is only part of the effort. I cannot say too often that everything we do throughout the day has a direct effect on the mind. I feel perplexed when I see someone put in sincere effort in meditation and then proceed to quarrel at breakfast, stomp out of the office in a huff at lunch, and not go home at all for dinner. I say bluntly: "You have undone all that you did so carefully in meditation." To keep going forward, we have to go on making our best effort to keep calm and kind throughout the day.

After dinner, too, even if the day has been rough, it does very little good to try to escape to the bowling alley or the dance hall. The desire to escape is natural enough, but there is really no place to run — and you would only be making the next day a little harder, by undoing a day's work of training. Instead, try to spend time with family or friends, building closer relationships, helping to lighten the burden of their day.

All this requires endless determination, as I am sure you are already aware. The first stages of meditation are rough going, and the only consolation I can offer is that below the surface of consciousness, the going gets even rougher. As you enter the immense, uncharted realm called the unconscious, there are so many imponderables you have to deal with, so many indecipherable scripts you have to learn to read. Even the most daring intellect looks around in vain for familiar landmarks and throws up its hands. "I don't understand this! There is nothing here that I can grasp, touch, see, or think about. I don't know what to do." The will lies down and goes to sleep, and every morning you have to try to rouse it again. This is a long, tough, terribly challenging battle.

But the rewards are infinite. If you read the annals of the great mystics, they seem to be having the time of their lives — dealing with intangibles, breaking codes that have never been broken, reading scripts that have never been made out. Every day there is a miracle in meditation. You have to fight against an enemy you cannot see, in a battle in which the lines cannot even be drawn. Yet you know you are learning to face these challenges; you know you are moving forward. That is all the inspiration you need, all the thrill you could ever hope to find. Throughout the day you do everything possible to clear your path into the unknown. And when you go to bed at night, you have a sense of having really lived — an awareness that no achievement in the external world can give.

I want you to know that this is just how I learned too. When I took to meditation, I was not living in seclusion in a cave on the Himalayas. I was a busy professor on a large campus in India, deeply interested in my students and in my subject, which was literature. In addition, I wrote a regular column for a national newspaper and spoke to sizable audiences over All-India Radio. I mention this simply to show that you do not have to drop out of society and go into hiding to pursue your spiritual goals. You do not have to slough your responsibilities so you can learn to meditate at your leisure — in fact, meditation is going to make you even more responsible. Meditation is a skill for *living*. You can draw on its benefits wherever you are — with your family, with your friends, on your campus, in your office, at your clinic, in your home. You can drive a taxi and still explore Infinity.

કે

Most of the difficulties people have in personal relations, at home and at work, arise from one ridiculous attitude: "If you give this much, that's all I'm going to give. If you are going to try to grab that, I'm going to try to grab it too." This peculiar stance is written into our human conditioning; that is why so much determination is required to change it. But living in freedom requires a complete reversal of perspective. Instead of asking "How much can I get?" we have to learn to ask "How much can I give?"

This is far more subtle than it may sound. Most of us need a long, long time to learn to ask this question in every aspect of our lives, even in our thoughts; it entails a complete turnabout in our direction of living. But that simple turnabout transforms our vision. The entire world looks different. Instead of feeling helpless in a world of hostile forces, you live in a world of hope, equal to any challenge; and by that transformation, you help everybody around you.

In the perspective of mysticism, most of us are still playing in the world as if we were children in a giant sandbox. We have our rattles, we hold on tightly to our Popsicles; for the vast majority of us, most of life is spent with toys. Figures like Sri Krishna, Christ, and the Buddha come to the edge of the sandbox and remind us gently, "Look, your hair is turning gray. Do you want to play here forever? There are vast worlds to be discovered." But often we reply, in effect, "Right, Lord. Just let me finish this one sand castle . . ."

I feel very happy now to see so many high school and college students coming to me to learn to meditate. They are extraordinarily fortunate, for they are getting out of the sandbox early in life. If we keep playing with pleasures and possessions for decades, before we realize it the sandbox becomes our universe. Then we have no thought for what we really are, who is within us, what is our destiny, whether life has any goal.

If this outlook sounds bleak, it is actually full of promise. It implies that we can always grow up. I am an inveterate optimist, and not of the naive variety either. If we take this compassionate view of human motivations, we won't consider the world around us hopeless. Throwing away our toys and growing up requires a great deal of determined effort, yet none of us has any reason to give up hope. That core of Infinity is still there, right within us, shining away just as brightly no matter how hard we try to look the other way. Saint Teresa, again, puts it very personally:

> Even when we are engaged in our worldly pastimes and businesses and pleasures and hagglings, this Lord of ours is so

anxious that we should desire him and strive after his companionship that he calls us ceaselessly, time after time, to approach him; . . . for His Majesty is quite prepared to wait even for years, especially when he sees we are persevering and have good desires. This is the most necessary thing here; if we have this, we cannot fail to gain greatly.

It should kindle our determination all the more to think how boundless his love for us must be, so anxious is he to draw us closer to him no matter how much we may tarry.

CHAPTER 13

Detachment

WHEN SCIENTISTS BEGAN contemplating the conquest of space, the first problem they encountered — a problem that had to be solved before they could make any headway at all — was how to get beyond the pull of the earth's gravity. A rocket has to build up a speed of twenty-five thousand miles per hour to escape this pull, and engineers quickly ran into a kind of "catch-22": to attain this speed, an ordinary rocket would have to be so large that its sheer weight would never allow it to escape the pull of gravity.

Yet the human spirit delights in overcoming obstacles. Undaunted, scientists finally came up with the idea of a multistage rocket, with one or more independent boosters attached. Each booster holds fuel, which it burns in one great leap upward. As soon as its fuel is expended, its job is done and the booster is dropped, freeing the spacecraft from the burden of its great weight.

Exploring inner space confronts us with a similar problem. What makes it so difficult to turn inward in meditation is the pull of objects and experiences outside us, the attraction of the physical world. Even memories, anxieties, plans, and so on draw their power from experiences of the senses: things we have felt, seen, heard, smelled, or tasted, which we want (or fear) to experience again.

This attraction is only natural, and there is nothing inherently wrong in it — just as gravity is natural, and there is nothing wrong with staying on earth. Problems arise only when we want more: new worlds to explore, a higher reality. Then we discover that the pull of our body, our senses, and our private, personal satisfactions is what keeps us earthbound, preventing us from soaring to those heights where we can look back and see that all of existence is one indivisible whole.

To rise above this pull, we have to build up a great deal of momentum. Just as in launching a rocket, immense power is required. But where are we to get such power? Space scientists can experiment with explosive mixtures such as liquid hydrogen and oxygen, but what do we use as human beings? The mystics give the answer: the power that drives a human being is desire. Our desires are our fuel.

I am full of admiration for the world's astronauts, who undergo such arduous training in their desire to go where no one has gone before. That desire is so great that it overrides all lesser predilections. For the sake of a few days in outer space and the thrill of seeing the earth floating free in a sea of stars, they are willing to learn all kinds of strange new skills and put up with endless deprivations.

To reach the Atman, shining like the full moon in the depths of consciousness, requires the same measure of dedication and training — and here, too, the secret is desire. If it is the power of our personal desires that keeps us earthbound, it is that same power, when released and harnessed, that will provide the fuel to launch us into higher consciousness.

To apply this we too need a booster rocket strategy, and the mystics of all religions have given us one, based on their own personal experience. In English it is called detachment: the art of withdrawing desire from lesser things, letting them fall away, so as to harness their power to reach the heights of what a human being can attain.

If a team of astronauts could travel to the Andromeda galaxy, our nearest neighbor in space, and come back again at the speed of light — this is where reason breaks down and the imagination boggles — by the time they got back, one million years would have elapsed on earth. Quite a little jaunt! Yet the astronauts themselves would be only fifty-six years older.

With statements like this, conventional concepts of time and space fly out the window. Yet even this is tame compared with travel in inner space. Once we pass beyond the pull of the outer world, the senses close down; awareness of the physical world falls away. The thought process slows greatly, and as the mind slows, time slows. When the mind finally loses itself in the Infinite, time stops. All identification with the body, senses, mind, and ego dissolves. We know then that we are neither body nor mind but pure spirit, and we are delivered from the realm of time and death into immortality.

This is the significance of the journey into the unconscious, and the very practical aim of cultivating detachment.

&

The practical implications of all this, I admit, may not sound reassuring. Living with a dissolved ego may sound like the road to oblivion. In practice, however, it is the road to love, vitality, and an overflowing, ever-present sense of joy.

Mahatma Gandhi was once asked by a Western journalist, "Can you give me the secret of your life in three words?" Gandhi, you know, could never pass up a challenge. "Three words?" he replied. "Of course: 'Renounce and enjoy!'"

If you really want to enjoy life, he meant, renounce all the personal demands you make on it. Give up trying to get people and circumstances to go your way. Learn to let go of your desires for personal pleasures and personal profit. Petty satisfactions like these are worth just pennies— or, as my young friend Julia would say, worth no more than a wooden nickel. When we let them go, we inherit the millions that are waiting for us like a trust fund in the depths of the unconscious.

What good business sense we have! "I can't accept your millions, Lord, because I'm afraid of losing this wooden nickel I have in my hand." This is where the spiritual teacher comes in, to set about the task of gradually persuading us that what we presently hold in our hand is w-o-o-d. "Your *head* is not made of wood," the teacher teases. "The nickel is. Throw it away!" And to allay our fears, he offers his personal example: "See, I have thrown it away. Look what I inherited!"

The Buddha, who almost never talked about himself, once admitted quietly, "I am the happiest of mortals. There is no one happier than I am." This is the joy for which every one of us is born. Not tuppenny-ha'penny pleasures, not tinsel delights or costume jewelry, but a jewel that is beyond price: the jewel hidden in the very depths of our hearts.

Detachment not only releases joy; it is also the secret of health. It is the best medical insurance in the world, and not only because it can keep us free from physical habits that sap our vitality. Most illness has a serious emotional element. With the help of friends in the medical profession, I hope to verify clinically that while there is an important place for physical measures in the treatment of disease, a mind at peace and a heart flooded with love can release healing powers that strengthen and revitalize the physical system. Strength can be regained even after years of emotional instability. In extreme cases, I believe, recovery can be brought about even from what seems a terminal illness.

Today, of course, it is widely appreciated that because of advances in medical knowledge, we can expect to live much longer than was reasonable at the beginning of our century. Men and women are often active in their sixties and seventies. And still we have a strange willingness to concede that this is a natural limit. I don't think so. We can push biological limits much further; we can lead lives that are not only longer but richer, more loving, and more productive. But the next steps in stretching the limits of human health and longevity, I believe, will not be in biotechnology. They will come from learning to govern the way we think and feel. Detachment is a longevity skill. Freedom from compulsive emotional entanglements is the best insurance against stress. More than that, by opening a window onto a fuller, loftier view of life than that dictated by self-interest, detachment brings a sense of purpose. Without a reason for living, the human being withers and dies inside. However paradoxical it may sound, it is detachment that enables us to give ourselves whole-heartedly to worthwhile work without ever getting depressed, despondent, or burned out — right into the last days of our lives.

Attachment means emotional entanglement, which takes a severe toll on vitality and therefore on health. You can check your detachment by a simple test: take a look at yourself and see how easily you get entangled in things up to your neck.

Most people who work hard, for example — which means most men and women in this country — bring their work home with them, yapping like a poodle at their heels. At the dinner table, when they sit thinking about their deadlines and responsibilities, the poodle is nestled under the chair, whining away. They curl up with it at night and dream about reports that haven't been filed, statistics that don't point to the right conclusions, mail that hasn't been responded to or that has been sent out with the wrong memo attached. This is the way with work. Detachment gives us the capacity to concentrate completely while on the job and to drop it completely when we walk out the door.

A detached worker is a reliable worker, a cheerful worker, a harmonious worker. And when you can drop your work completely at the end of the day, you arrive home ready to give all your love to your family and friends. You feel fresh, relaxed. You have no need to give vent to the kind of frustration that millions of good people air: "Leave me alone. I've had a miserable day!" Mahatma Gandhi worked fifteen hours a day for fifty years for all of us who want a politically free world. When he was asked,

"Don't you want a vacation, Mr. Gandhi?" he said quietly, "I'm always on vacation." It wasn't a flippant reply; he meant every word of it. So don't content yourself with two weeks in July or two weeks at a ski resort in January. You deserve three hundred and sixty-five days of vacation, and that is exactly what detachment can give you.

Detachment brings this kind of protection at every stage of life. Many of the physical problems associated with old age, for example, are not at all a necessary part of aging. The fact that they are common does not mean they are inexorable. Not only senility but even certain physical problems may well have more to do with life-style and thought-style than with changes triggered by some biological clock.

As researchers have observed, we have focused so much on "ordinary aging" — what happens to the majority — that we have ignored "successful aging," which we can observe in men and women like Mahatma Gandhi, George Bernard Shaw, and Mother Teresa, who grow in wisdom and vitality right into the last days of a long, creative, fulfilling life. I grant you that in the evening of your life you may not be able to compete successfully on Centre Court at Wimbledon. But every one of us can enjoy the vitality, resourcefulness, and unerring judgment that come from a heart full of love and a vast reservoir of experience.

Even the current economic crisis has a positive side, for it too can teach us detachment. I think it was Will Rogers who advised, "Buy land. They ain't makin' that stuff no more!" On the other hand, Tolstoy has a haunting story titled "How Much Land Does a Man Need?" He ends with a rather grim answer: six feet. Terrible but true. Isn't there a saying in this country, "You can't take it with you"? Most of us act as if we *can* take it with us. The "frenzy of consumerism" has probably never been more frantic. Whatever our philosophy, we are saying loudly with our actions, "If I want something, I am going to get it and hold on to it, no matter what."

This is natural but futile. I am sure the Buddha would come right out and say it: "Man, you're not going to be taking *any* of this along! Why don't you accumulate something you *can* take with you?" When I first read this in the Dhammapada, I said out loud, "Blessed One, you took the words right out of my heart!" What can we take with us? Kind thoughts, kind words, kind deeds. All these add up, even if we believe in no afterlife at all. The quality of our thoughts and words and deeds, the Buddha says, is what decides our life. Our future life is what we are deciding this very minute.

Please do not misunderstand me! There is nothing wrong with having material possessions or even with making money, so long as it is not at the expense of life. But without detachment, it is not possible even to enjoy things and use them wisely. I am not pleading for poverty but praising simplicity. If I were to write a book to follow E. F. Schumacher's, it would be called "Simple Is Beautiful." To lead a simple life in reasonable comfort, with a minimum of possessions, ranks high among the arts of living. It leaves us the time, resources, and freedom of mind we need for the things that give life value: loving, helping, serving, and giving.

ð

In English the word *detachment* sounds passive, callous, unfeeling. Yet it is just the opposite, and the best way to see this is to look at its application in personal relationships.

In Sanskrit, we have two words that are often translated as "love" — two words with a world of difference between them, and the difference is detachment. *Prema* is pure love, in which I want nothing but your happiness. Your joy *is* my joy. *Kama*, on the other hand, is self-centered personal attachment, generally with romantic overtones. In the language of kama, "I love you" means "you please me." Most of us need no formal introduction to kama. Selfish attachment is what holds most novels together, what most popular songs are based on, what most films depict in graphic detail.

It is discouragingly easy to mistake selfish attachment for love if we do not really know what love is. If you want

to see some of the greatest lovers of all time, don't look to
Romeo or Juliet; look at Saint Francis of Assisi, or lovely
Saint Teresa of Avila. All you need do is read Teresa's au-
tobiographical accounts to know that she lived in the
empyrean of love. What a wonderful paradox: to know
what love means, we have to turn to men and women who
we say have "renounced the world"!

Listen to Jacob Boehme, the "cosmic cobbler" of medieval Germany, as he tells us us how he knew when he was
in love — eternal love:

> No life can express, nor tongue so much as name, what this
> enflaming, all-consuming love of God is. It is brighter than
> the sun, it is sweeter than anything called sweet; it is stronger
> than all strength; it is more nutrimental than food, more
> cheering to the heart than wine, and more pleasant than all
> the joy and pleasantness of the world. Whoever obtaineth it
> is richer than any monarch on earth; and he who getteth it is
> nobler than any emperor can be, and more potent and abso-
> lute than all power and authority.

Boehme is talking about love in the truest sense. The
mark of true love is as simple as it is rare: it is detachment,
not from other people but from our own ego, from the
tangle of personal motives that makes us seek happiness in
making others conform to our desires. Detachment and
love go hand in hand. When all selfish attachments are
gone, what is left is pure love. The other person is so dear
to you that you never have to ask yourself the question,
"What is she going to give me?"—in the way of respect, of
affection, of loyalty. Once you efface that question from
your vocabulary completely, you and that person are no
longer separate; both of you are one. That is what love
means.

All of us begin the quest for love with a great deal of
selfish attachment. That is human nature. But with the
help of meditation and the allied disciplines we can
diminish this selfish element day by day, by putting the
welfare of those around us first and our own personal
predilections last.

But practicing detachment in personal relationships does not come easily. No other arena of life is more challenging. Disrupted relationships are endemic today, and not because people are immoral or because they don't care about one another; they just don't know how to develop detachment. If you cannot stand back from your own pleasure and profit, you cannot help manipulating other people. Naturally, this kind of manipulation corrodes loyal relationships of any kind. It leads to their speedy end, as we can see in the lives of millions of lonely people today.

When you practice detachment continuously — at home, at work, among friends, and especially with difficult people – you will find how much security it brings you in your relationships. A spiritually detached person, which to me means a very loving person, will never allow relationships to degenerate to stimulus and response. The test is simple: Even if you are angry with me, can I stay calm and loving with you and help you overcome your anger? If you persist in disliking me, can I continue to like you? For it is when you dislike me that I have all the more reason to be loyal to you, to show you what loyalty really means.

This problem of disliking people, which is a very common one today, is essentially a problem of disliking the images we have formed of them. It is a reflection on us rather than on those we do not like. For in almost all human relationships, we see others not as they really are but as *we* are. To a suspicious person, everybody seems suspect; to a resentful person, every action is worthy of resentment. Similarly, to a loving person, everybody is worthy of love; every occasion is an opportunity to practice love. It is not that situations never get difficult when you are detached, or that people are never unpleasant. But the choice of response is in your hands. All of us can develop the detachment not to react to the way we are treated. This is the easiest, most effective way to solve problems in human relationships.

I once read a good aphorism from Buckminster Fuller. "We are not nouns," he says pointedly; "we are verbs."

People who are content with rigid images of others are thinking of themselves and others as nouns, as things. Those who keep trying to get closer to others, to understand and appreciate them more all the time, are verbs: active, creative, dynamic, able to change themselves and to make changes in the world they live in.

Here is the practical difference. When we don't like somebody, we say, "He upsets me. I'm not going to go near him." That relationship is static; it has no chance of improving. On the other hand, when we can go against our dislikes, we can actually enjoy the opportunity such a person presents us. Just imagine the freedom! We enjoy being with people who like us, of course, but we can also enjoy being with people who don't like us. Sometimes I think Gandhiji used to look forward to this kind of opportunity, because he knew it would draw up from within him the deeper creative resources he needed for his work.

Without this kind of freedom, "love" is more an inclination that comes and goes like the wind. When your girlfriend is catering to you, doing all the things you like, you say you love her. But when she turns around and does something that irritates you, you blurt out, "Get lost!" Doesn't this happen all too often?

To love truly, you must be able to love when things are going your way and equally well when things are *not* going your way. This is the test of detachment. After all, when your partner is being especially nice to you, it's easy to be pleasant in return. It is when she goes out of her way to offend you that you should not walk out. That is just the time to sit by her side and for every unkind word she utters, as Jesus says, give her seven words that are kind. For every shove she gives you, try to move that much closer.

When I came to this country, I heard a popular song with a refrain that struck me as rather odd: "Oh, what a beautiful mornin'! Oh, what a beautiful day! I've got a beautiful feelin' everything's goin' my way." If somebody sings that to me, I will retort, "When are you going to grow up?" I appreciate the person who can come rubbing her hands together happily and say, "Everything's going *your* way" — and then add truthfully, "What a beautiful day!" That person is tremendously secure, immensely loving. She can be completely happy just because someone else is happy; and when others are unhappy, she will share their sorrow too — not with maudlin sentimentality but with the determination to help and console, which is the deepest source of joy.

To do this at home in the morning, at work throughout the day, and then in the evening among family and friends, you have to have a good measure of detachment from yourself. These are challenges that can appeal to us deeply: the "acts of will" that Saint Teresa of Avila says the Lord wants of us. They *are* difficult, but they can be practiced, and to great effect. To grow to our full potential in love, we need to try every day to develop a little more detachment from ourselves. Those who get angry and walk out, who get resentful and won't sit at the same table with others, are refusing to try to grow. Their problem can be solved very simply, to the benefit of everyone around them: they need to practice detachment every day in every situation, in every relationship.

This reminds me of a beautiful incident from the life of Saint Thérèse of Lisieux, a young woman of our own century of whom I am very fond. In her convent was a certain nun who had a knack for alienating others. She seemed always to be waiting for someone to upset. Naturally her sisters tended to avoid her — even Thérèse, the Little Flower, as she is sweetly called. No one meant to be unkind; it was just that avoiding the unpleasant is so natural.

Then, with a shock, Thérèse realized what she had been doing. With her, as with Saint Francis — here is the mark of a saint! — to understand was to act. Immediately she began to make a point of giving her irritating sister a smile, answering her with kind words, doing little things to help her: although inside, she confesses, she used to wince with the effort.

One day, in a moment of marvelous simplicity, that nun stopped Thérèse and surprised her with a question. "Sister, whenever we meet, you always give me such a sweet smile. Will you please tell me what attracts you so much to me?"

"Ah!" Thérèse confides to us. "How could I tell her that what attracts me is Jesus, hidden in the depths of her soul – Jesus who makes sweet that which is most bitter!"

Jesus had taught her, "Bless them that curse you. Do good to them that hate you." That is love at its greatest. In order to love like this, we cannot be attached to ourselves. It is because we think so much about ourselves that we strike back, show resentment, speak harshly, move away.

Jesus' words do not mean agreeing with everything people say or supporting whatever they do. In my role as a spiritual teacher, I sometimes have to oppose people I love. Yet I do it tenderly, and I haven't lost a single friend. On the contrary, my friends say, "Here is somebody who will stand by me through thick and thin. If I make a mistake, he'll support me, but he'll do his best not to let me make that mistake again. If I'm going astray, he'll bar my way with loving arms."

As Shakespeare says, "Love bears it out even to the edge of doom." This is the secret of loving. Let me repeat, for a long, long time everybody finds it difficult. Everybody finds it distressing. But when you go to bed after a day of practicing this kind of love, you know that you have grown. You can stand against the wall and see that you have grown a full inch in spiritual stature. Inch by inch, day by day, you can grow until your head is crowned with the stars. That is our human destiny – the destiny for which all of us have been born.

Discrimination

DURING MY DAYS as a professor of English literature, one writer with whom I felt a special kinship was Gilbert Keith Chesterton. Not only did he do keen studies of favorites of mine such as Robert Browning and Charles Dickens, but he wrote a fascinating portrait of Saint Francis of Assisi which shows that Chesterton had some personal grounding in matters of the spirit. You can see this even in those rattling good detective stories he gave us, featuring the redoubtable Father Brown.

On one occasion, it seems, friends of Chesterton's were complaining that people today have nothing to believe in. "The real problem," Chesterton replied, "is that when you don't have something to believe in, you will believe in anything at all."

This is our great contemporary tragedy. If something is presented seductively, if it appeals to our society's carefully cultivated taste for profit or pleasure, most of us will believe in anything that comes along. Millions of people of all ages and occupations, out of intentions which for the most part could not be called wrong, are entangled in activities that in the long run will injure their health, impair their peace of mind, inflict suffering on their families, darken their prospects, and eventually threaten the very life of our society — all because, in the depths of their hearts, they lack something to believe in that is loftier and more meaningful than personal pleasure and profit.

Contrast this picture with the scene five thousand years ago on the banks of the Ganges. The sages of ancient India used to pray every morning as the tropical sun rose in glory:

> *Ya ātmadā baladā yasya vishva*
> *Upāsate prashisham yasya devāh*

> "To that radiant Being, who gives life and strength,
> I offer all my desires, all that I am."

This shining Being within is what gives meaning to life. Nothing in the world of change outside us can provide the abiding purpose that we seek. "He is the source of my strength, my very self," this prayer implies; "so I owe my life to him. Everything I do, everything I desire, everything I am, should go to serve him in the rest of his creation. Understanding this gives purpose to life; practicing this brings fulfillment."

Sanskrit describes this core of divinity as *satyam, shivam, sundaram:* the source of truth, of goodness, and of beauty. The seas surge with the flow of his love; the mountains reflect his glory. All the loveliness we see in nature is his. Yet although we may admire the beauties of his garden, the mystics say, very, very few of us actually seek to discover the Gardener, who dwells in the heart of every creature.

Different religions use different names for this aspect of divinity which is the very core of our being: Krishna, Christ, the Buddha, Allah, the Divine Mother. But the reality referred to is one and the same. In Sanskrit the term is simple and universal: Atman, the Self, radiant, loving, immortal, infinite, who is the same in all beings, in all creatures, in all of life.

"The soul has two eyes," says Meister Eckhart: "one looking inwards and the other looking outwards. It is the inner eye of the soul that looks into essence and takes being directly from God." It is because we do not know how to

look to this shining Being inside us that we try to light up
our dim lives from outside in any way we can. Not knowing how to turn inward, we look for meaning and
fulfillment in the fickle realm of sensory experience.

Those who are sensitive to what goes on inside them
know how much of this effort is generated by a nagging
sense of desperation, of emptiness within. Such is the nature of the human being, such is our very constitution, that
we *have* to have a purpose greater than the endless struggle
to satisfy personal desires. We have to believe in something
more lasting than creature comforts. Otherwise we will
eventually feel driven to do anything, try anything, to find
fulfillment — as Chesterton implies, to do anything at all.

We need, in short, a central force to hold us together;
otherwise we fly apart, pursuing our separate goals. The
Sanskrit word for this force is one of the oldest and most
meaningful in the Upanishads: *dharma,* "law," — the law of
unity, that life is one indivisible whole. The Buddha did
not talk about God; he said simply, "*Esa dhammo sanatano:*
the fact that all of us are one and indivisible is an eternal
law." Unity is the very law of life. In that law lies our
growth; in it lies our future; in it lies our fulfillment. And
today, in the world of medicine, we are discovering that in
unity also lies our health, our longevity, our vitality. When
we live just for ourselves, we are stunting our own growth
and courting illness. It is in living for all that we rise to our
full potential of vibrant, vital, creative action.

Much of the art of living, then, rests on the rare ability
to discriminate between what is in harmony with this central law of life and what violates it. To act wisely, we must
see clearly. "Does this particular choice bring me closer to
my partner or my family? Does it resolve a conflict, foster
clean air, bring peace to my mind or to people around
me?" If the answer to such questions is yes, that course of
action is in harmony with the unity of life. If the answer is
no, it is not — however pleasant it may be.

To grow spiritually, we need both the detachment to see
clearly and the discrimination to know what is of lasting

value — and, of course, the willpower — the determination–to put our insight into action. Discrimination is the third of my three *D*s, and it flows directly from the second, detachment. Discrimination is pure, detached love in action.

Without discrimination, by contrast, "anything goes." The only basis for choice is personal conditioning — likes and dislikes. One of the grimmest warnings in the Sanskrit scriptures states, "Lack of discrimination is the source of the greatest danger" — to health, to security, to personal relations, to life itself.

Despite its tremendous achievements, one of my lover's quarrels with modern industrial civilization is that it is so lacking in discrimination, that it cannot see how its choices and values are violating the unity of life. In focusing on manipulating the world outside us, it has lost sight of the world within; yet only there can we find meaning, purpose, and value. More than any other quality of modern life, it is essentially this lack of discrimination that is sending our world on a collision course with disaster.

ૐ

In daily living, discrimination means making wise choices — knowing what to do and what not to do, not so much in moral terms as in terms of where our choices lead.

One of the most stirring of the Sanskrit scriptures, the Katha Upanishad, uses two marvelous words to help us see which course of action will lead to trouble in the long run and which will lead to detached, loving living. I say "marvelous" because these words apply to every choice, in every circumstance, so they dispel the haze that often surrounds a difficult situation. Wherever you have a choice, ask yourself this question: "Which is *preya,* that which pleases, and which is *shreya,* the long-term good?"

Preya is what we like, what pleases us, what offers immediate gratification to senses, feelings, or self-will. Shreya is simply what works out best in the end. Preya is the "pleasure principle": doing what feels good, whatever the consequences. Shreya means choosing the best consequences, whether it feels good or not — often forgoing a temporary pleasure for the sake of a lasting benefit.

Junk food is one of the clearest illustrations of preya: sugar, salt, and saturated fat so fast and easy that you don't even have to sit down for it. The consequences are equally clear. Or look at exercise: "no pain, no gain." Training and toning the body often is not pleasant. We do it for the sake of its long-range benefits — because later we will really feel good in a deeper, longer-lasting, more satisfying way. That is shreya, choosing what is best.

When we learn how to look for it, we see that this choice between preya and shreya comes up every moment, in virtually everything we do. There is no escaping it. The moment dawn breaks, the choices begin: "Shall I get up for my meditation, or shall I pull the blanket over my head and stay in bed a little longer?" It starts there, and it goes on until you fall asleep at night.

Early morning, therefore, have your meditation right on time. It sets the tone for the rest of the day. The Bhagavad Gita, in a verse that is etched on my heart, assures us that regular meditation will protect us from life's gravest dangers. "*Svalpamapasya dharmasya trāyate mahato bhayāt:* Even a little meditation will guard you against the greatest fears": against physical ailments, emotional problems, disrupted relationships, spiritual alienation. Most critical, perhaps, meditation slowly opens our eyes and hearts to the needs of those around us. That is discrimination, and I know of no better protection against the mistaken choices that can so burden life with guilt and regret.

After meditation, of course, more choices come in a flurry, generally at the breakfast table. With all the conditioning of the media, where eating is concerned, right choices are not easy. Food has become a kind of religion, and business is quick to cash in on it. To choose wisely, your senses must listen to you. That is the essential prerequisite. And for your senses to listen to you, your mind must listen to you. That is why, as you train your mind in meditation, your eating habits come under your control. Likes and dislikes begin to change, and choices open up everywhere.

Yet discrimination, of course, extends not only to eating but to everything. In the Sanskrit scriptures, we are said to eat through all the senses. Just as we learn to be discriminating about what we put into our mouths, we learn to be vigilant about the books and magazines we read, the movies and television we absorb, the conversation we indulge in, the company we keep: in short, in everything we do and say. Ultimately this extends even to what we think. We have a choice in all these things; that is what is meant by intentional living.

Let me illustrate with reading. Having spent the first half of my life in the world of books, I can speak about them with some authority. There was even a time when I thought the Lord could be found in the lower stacks of the library. That was a phase I had to go through, being a university man. Today, because I am involved in publishing, I still look at bookstore shelves and book-trade journals with great interest. But I have to confess that I see very few books worth reading; and when I look at some of the magazines and tabloids on display in supermarkets, I envy my grandmother her illiteracy. It has come to such a pass.

Even where highly recommended books are concerned, we have to be exceedingly judicious about what we put into our minds. The fact that a book has become a bestseller is no guarantee at all of quality. I am not talking about morality now but simply about the effect on the mind. When you are training a puppy, you don't try to teach it limits for an hour and then say, "All right, you're off duty now. Go do whatever you like for the rest of the day." It is the same with training the mind. Why spend half an hour every morning in meditation, going through the agony of teaching an unruly mind to be calm and clear, and then go out and stir up all its appetites again in the name of relaxation?

Some years ago, a man who honestly thought he was doing people a service wrote a best-selling book on sex.

The subtitle might well have been "A Guide to Disrupted Relationships and a Bloated Ego." His theme was simple: "Your needs come first. Don't hesitate to impose them on others; everybody will be happier for it." When has this ever worked?

Anybody who takes this kind of advice seriously is going to become more lonely, more frustrated, and more estranged. Physical appetites can never be satisfied for long; the more we want, the less they can be fulfilled. Gradually the mind becomes unruly in everything, and other people become things that either please or hinder us. Then, where two people sincerely sought love, they find only anger, bitterness, and regret. Yet the books and magazines and movies go on promising: satisfaction lies in sex, and it's just around the corner; just try again . . .

Many years ago, for the Fulbright orientation program, I spent a beautiful summer month at the University of Kansas, where I visited the home of a colleague who had a twelve- or thirteen-year-old daughter. In the course of the evening I got acquainted with the girl and said, "Let's see what you are reading." After looking over the row of books piled up on her desk for the summer vacation, I went privately to her father, just as I would have done in India. "Do you know what kind of books your daughter is reading?" I asked.

"Oh, sure," he said casually, as if amused by my provincial Indian attitude. "This is a free country, you know."

I had already heard this a few times before. "By the way," I said, "I notice you lock the bathroom cabinet. Is that an American custom?"

"No," he laughed. "That's where we keep dangerous drugs, so the kids don't get into them."

"There are drugs that injure the body," I said, "and there are books that injure the mind."

To him, I suppose, this must have sounded censorious. But just as a physician understands what drugs can do to the body, I understand what sense impressions and potent images do to the mind. That is my field. It disturbs me deeply that most of our children have little guidance in what goes into their minds, and I will tell you why. In our area we have a popular daily that boasts on its masthead, "Sex and Crime." Every day a big dose of both is offered. When this is poured in over and over again, sex and crime is what a person is going to think about. He or she is being drugged — and no street drug is more addictive.

Today, of course, my young friend's summer reading would look tame compared with what is available to teenagers now. Books and magazines are much more explicit, and potent mind-drugs are available at the touch of a button, acted out for us on the screen so that everything is reduced to its lowest level. The real problem raised by this kind of mass distribution of mind-drugs is spelled out in two terrible verses in the Gita:

> When you keep thinking about sense objects,
> Attachment comes. Attachment breeds desire,
> The lust of possession which, when thwarted,
> Burns to anger. Anger clouds the judgment,
> And robs you of the power to learn from past mistakes.
> Lost is the discriminative faculty, and your life
> Is utter waste.

As our minds fill up with junk thoughts and junk feelings, we get addicted to them. We lose our discrimination, and as these junk thoughts fail to satisfy — as they must — the craving for them becomes more and more acute. But we are hooked: we can't get them out of our heads, out of our relationships. Is it merely coincidence that angry, frustrated teenagers are turning to just what that tabloid touts . . . sex and crime?

X-rated material aside, consider ordinary TV fare. If a child spends an hour a day with a parent and five or six hours watching the fantasies of MTV and the so-called realism of soap operas, what images of people and of personal relationships are going to fill that child's mind? What makes up the bulk of his or her experience? Whether we like it or not, this is the world that child will live in; those experiences are teaching that child how to act.

There was a time when, saying these things, I felt my

voice was crying in the wilderness. Today I am very glad to say that I am not alone. Excellent books like Marie Wynn's *Unplugging the Plug-In Drug* relate the experience of many, many families who have "gone straight": either locked the television in the basement or thrown it out altogether. After a short period of deprivation, people discover suddenly that they have time again — time for being together, time for doing the things they want which somehow got crowded out. In addition, for anyone who is meditating, I doubt that any single step could make more difference than getting the television habit under control.

One gentle, effective way children can be weaned from the set is for their father or mother to take a good book and read to them. If that sounds old-fashioned, try it. Many families of former TV addicts will tell you that it works. Younger children love to have a story read or told to them, and if older children want to read to themselves, encourage them and set an example. We need to educate their tastes, show them how to appreciate stories with depth, sensitivity, and strength of character rather than just action — and most parents find that in educating their children's tastes, they educate their own as well. There are many good books available today, not only the time-tested classics but good stories by contemporary authors, and no end of books that explore science and culture in ways young people can understand. I have seen children coming to ask for such books. They won't be content with the cheap substitutes our mass media try to force down their minds.

But we need to set them a good example with our own reading too. There you can do no better than to turn to the mystical tradition. It is a whole world of beautiful literature, inspiring, practical, nourishing, strengthening. These are words that have endured the passage of centuries. In the Hindu tradition we have magnificent epics, the *Ramayana* and the *Mahabharata,* which cannot be surpassed for drama, adventure, character, and spiritual insight. Most Hindu children grow up on these stories, which offer noble role models and teach the basic laws of life in the midst of high entertainment.

Every spiritual tradition has its literature, full of poetry and the passionate desire to communicate what words cannot contain, where men and women who have soared to the heights of human experience try to convey to us what they have discovered and what they encountered along the way.

Every day, in everything, we have a choice. Nobody can say, "I'm not free to choose." Those two words from the Upanishads can always help us see our choices clearly: preya, that which is pleasant but which probably benefits nobody, even ourselves; and shreya, that which is of lasting benefit to all. Shall I reply curtly to her rude remark, or shall I speak kindly? Shall I spend the afternoon doing something I like, or shall I work at something that helps a few others? Everywhere we have choices like these, and discrimination comes when we start choosing what brings lasting benefit even at the cost of a few private, personal satisfactions.

As you start doing this, you will feel the chains of conditioning on your wrists and ankles slowly falling away. Do you remember Charles Dickens's *Christmas Carol*? In an eerie scene, which I still recall vividly from the movie, the ghost of Scrooge's old partner Marley comes into Scrooge's bedroom rattling his chains. Scrooge looks up and exclaims in fright, "Marley! What happened to you? How did you come by all those chains?" And Alec Guinness, with that sardonic grin of his, replies grimly, "I made them all myself. Link by link. Every one of them."

That is what selfish pursuits become in the long run: chains. Though we never intended it, though we may have taken it up only as recreation, every selfish activity becomes a chain. At the outset we have no intention of disliking and avoiding and deprecating and manipulating. But in the end we find ourselves with very little choice. In matters of this magnitude, an ounce of discrimination is worth pounds and pounds of the effort it takes to cut off chains with a dainty jeweler's file, which is the kind of work that is required when selfish habits are allowed to grow rigid and strong.

ટ≻

"I found thee not, O Lord, without, because I erred in seeking thee without that wert within." Augustine speaks for us all. When we do not know that life's fulfillment lies within us, we cannot help reaching for what is outside. And the more these attempts fail to satisfy, the more insecure we become. That is why so many spend their lives in some kind of hoarding: money, possessions, pleasures, memories, always trying to reassure themselves with something more. Advertisers cash in on this desire every day. Those copywriters on Madison Avenue really know what touches us. They must be sitting over their cups of espresso every morning and saying, "Just call those cigarettes 'More.' You don't have to say more of what, just 'More.' Everybody will respond."

Do you remember *Fiddler on the Roof,* when Tevye exclaims, "Lord, if money is a curse, strike me so hard that I may never recover from it!" This is probably a universal sentiment. It is the basis of the confusion in which civilization so often functions: make as much money as you can; it will make you happy, secure, loved, and respected.

Of course, money has a place in life, even in the spiritual life. But to ascribe to money these impossible magic qualities, to make it the measure of things or the very goal of life, is to disinherit ourselves from the divine trust fund we all have stored up inside. Our real wealth is our inner resources, which are infinite because the core of our personality is divine. And the purpose of life is not to accumulate physical tokens of wealth but to mine these deeper resources for the good of all. That is the supreme goal of our existence and the only source of lasting value. Meister Eckhart, one of the greatest mystics the world has produced, puts this in memorable words:

> Nature's purpose is neither food, nor drink, nor clothing, nor comfort, nor anything else from which God is left out. Whether you like it or not, whether you know it or not, secretly nature seeks and hunts and tries to ferret out the track in which God may be found.

Most of our daily activities, by contrast, are rooted in the religion of "more": more wealth, more possessions, more production, bigger cash flow. We even evaluate nations in these terms, as if national quantities of goods and wealth had anything to do with the quality of life for individual human beings.

Developing countries, for example, are told to do anything they can to increase their GNP, even though it may benefit no one in that country but a wealthy few. Borrowing Eckhart's phrase, I would advise any country to interpret "GNP" very differently: "Do everything you can to further Great Nature's Purpose." Translated into economic terms, this means not more corporate cash crops but, first, enough food for those who grow it. It means not more goods for export but productive work for people where they live. It means not more economic activity for the nation but *meaningful* economic activity for that nation's *people:* work, goods, and services that actually improve the quality of life for individual men, women, and children. I like very much that statement "Food for people, not for profit." Everything should be for people; that is what the unity of life means in practice.

How farsighted old Eckhart was, back in medieval Germany! In the end, Nature itself is teaching us the first lesson of discrimination: that "more" can only be sought within, and trying to satisfy infinite appetites in a finite world is not merely futile but disastrous. "More, more, more" simply cannot be had forever, not at any expense. Every material resource is limited; many today are in critically short supply. Clean air is scarce. Cities and states stage courtroom battles over water. Essential minerals, their natural availability further hampered by global politics, are being used up at a prodigious rate. Abruptly we are being forced to learn that everything is limited. Every resource has to be used wisely, thriftily, even if we do manage to slow our accelerating rate of "growth."

This is not simply a matter of economics. It is a clear sign that we need to look for a wiser religion than materialism. The idea of growth for growth's sake, which has been the driving motive behind civilization for hundreds of years, can now be likened to what one writer calls a "creed of cancer." We are pushing the natural physical limits of our environment to such an extent that we can safely go no further — if, indeed, we have not already gone too far. "Lack of discrimination is the source of the greatest danger": we are at a precipice, and over the edge lies disaster.

Thoughtful observers all over the world today echo what twenty years ago almost no one believed: that discrimination lies in wanting less from the world outside us, and that great dangers can arise from wanting more and more. The whole world today is held ransom by the stockpiles of the deadliest "growth industry" in history, the nuclear arms race. Yet we go on adding to our bank accounts, our collectibles, our "survival stores," the lists of pleasures we have enjoyed, as if by keeping busy, busy, busy we can escape what common sense says should dictate the first priority of us all: the fact that in half an hour's time, life as we know it can simply come to an end.

Some years ago a distinguished biologist propounded a theory called "lifeboat ethics" in an attempt to enlighten ignorant altruists on the subject of world hunger. The idea is simple: the wealthier nations are in a lifeboat with limited supplies; the poor nations are floundering in the sea. "Obviously," he points out, "not everybody can be saved." If we try to put everyone in the boat, everybody will lose. Better — even, he says, more humane — to let die the millions who cannot save themselves and help the few nations who may be able to achieve self-sufficiency. We might begin, he adds candidly, with those whose survival is important to our own national self-interest.

Many people, I am glad to say, immediately assailed this as not lifeboat ethics but gunboat ethics. Yet the principle behind it continues to influence national policy, simply because both focus on the fatal fallacy that one nation — or one race, or one individual — can achieve its welfare at another's expense. This distinguished scientist, I would say, missed the point of his own metaphor. We are all in that lifeboat, "spaceship Earth," and the "deathboat ethics" he describes cannot help but lead to throwing others overboard, for the simple reason that it is based on saving not the lives of many but the life-style of a few.

I mention this theory because the same kind of reasoning comes up also in discussions of nuclear war. The main reason we say such a war is unthinkable, Herman Kahn once said, is "because we are crazy." To be sane, we should acknowledge that of course it is "thinkable" and plan accordingly. No one really has any idea what this means, but on the basis of Hiroshima and guesswork the experts estimate that perhaps twenty million people — not even soldiers on a battlefield, but ordinary citizens — would die immediately in even a limited nuclear exchange. Social and economic chaos would follow, and deaths in the hundreds of thousands would accumulate from aftereffects in the years to come. But simple arithmetic, Dr. Kahn pointed out, still leaves sixty to a hundred million people who might survive in one form or another. If we can save what we need to rebuild factories and pump up our GNP again — and, of course, rearm the nation — we could reasonably claim to have "won."

This, too, is a remarkably candid comment on values. Who is this "we"? First priority in the nuclear lifeboat, of course, goes to saving our federal and military leaders — although it is difficult to say who they would lead, and whether they had really done that good a job. Next comes protecting and rebuilding our capacity to turn out material goods, without which America would supposedly not be America. Least important, apparently, are the nameless, expendable casualties — the men, women, and children who happen to live in or around Washington, Dallas, San Francisco, Seattle, Detroit, Chicago, Boston, New York, and dozens of other cities that are known to be targets in a nuclear war.

You can see that when I say this is "deathboat ethics," I am not trying to be clever. Sacrificing others is always the result when getting and holding are valued more than individual lives. Shreya, the long-term benefit of all, urges,

"Life first. Everything should be for the sake of life." Preya says, "Me first" — whether "me" is a person, a corporation, or the "national interest" which so often seems to include the people we know.

It is important to answer the preposterous proposals of deathboat ethics by doing our homework and presenting positive, practical alternatives. Discriminating between preya and shreya is always a good place to begin: What is in the real interests of the whole? A workable answer needs to include the interests of everyone involved. To shed this nuclear nightmare, we have to change the attitudes which lead to war — beginning with the assumption that we are all adversaries in life, fighting over a larger share of the pie. "There is enough on earth for everyone's need," Gandhi said, "but not enough for everyone's greed." Discrimination means understanding that the welfare of each of us is part of the welfare of us all.

The vast majority of us, of course, are not so greedy that we would choose to let others suffer to get what we desire. But when a person gets wrapped up in personal interests, other people become shadows. And as far as most of us are concerned, our love is constrained to what we can see. If we are not aware of anybody suffering on our block, or on our own side of town, we feel content not to think about it further; our thoughts are already full. The plight of those living in desperate conditions in the inner city districts of our own home towns does not touch us appreciably. Nor does the sight of so many of our young people, our hope for the future, feeling they have nothing to pour their energy into except the search for chemical thrills and aimless acts of violence.

My wife and I often used to visit San Francisco, which Herb Caen called affectionately "Baghdad by the Bay." I liked to quote his remark that everybody really has two home towns, his own and San Francisco. But in the past few years I have had trouble believing he was talking about the same city. A recent opinion piece in the *Chronicle*, written by an out-of-state visitor, asked the same question I had: how is it that with so much idealism and enterprise, such vast resources of money and talent, we cannot alleviate the dreadful conditions in which so many of our citizens live?

Thousands of good people today, I am told, live in boredom and loneliness, looking for some kind of meaning in their lives. Why not pour at least a little of that time and energy into making life better for the homeless street-dwellers in the cities near them, for the runaway young, for the abandoned elderly who literally have to choose each month between food and heating? For many, the answer is pitiful: This religion of grabbing, of "looking out for number one," does not allow for fellow-feeling. It only deadens our sensitivity, building the walls of loneliness and alienation higher and higher.

And these are our own people, after all, living right in our midst; how much more difficult, then, to remember those in Africa, Asia, and Latin America, the millions of children who go to bed hungry and get up dreading another day. When you have the kind of love the mystics speak of, it will give a quiet sense of joy to take a little less from life so that those who need it can have more. You will want to devote at least part of your day, part of your time and energy and financial resources, to causes that help people in critical need. "To that shining Being, whom I see in everyone, I offer all that I have, all that I am."

❧

I have been reading a collection of articles by historians, biologists, and anthropologists who speak of great stages in human evolution. The first stage, they say, was biological. The second, which includes the present era, is cultural. The symbol of the first stage was the hand; of the second, the head. But now it is time for a tremendous step forward into a third stage, which might be called the era of the heart.

"The time has come," these writers conclude, "when we must have a purpose in life or run the risk of perishing as a species." This is the latest discovery of some of our most outstanding thinkers. Last night, after reading this, I found myself chuckling quietly. I couldn't help myself.

Meister Eckhart's words were echoing in my ears with a bittersweet tone: "Whether you know it or not, whether you like it or not," your whole personality, your very life, is searching for that shining Being in your heart.

We find we need a higher purpose now just to be able to discriminate between permanent values and passing fascinations — science aside, technology aside. Two and a half cars to the average household: whom does it help? The atmosphere? The children whom experts warn to stay indoors on smoggy days? The native beauty and lush resources of our country? The papers boast about having twenty million vehicles on the roads in our golden state of California. Why not make wiser use of fewer vehicles? That would be real progress. Clean rapid transit systems are within reach if we choose. Buses and van pools can cut traffic to a fraction. But has it been progress for travel to be so cheap and easy? And what has been the full cost? Instead of adding to the highway statistics and the smog, why not spend more time at home, where our time and love are so badly needed? That is what discrimination means in transportation: fewer cars (and smaller ones), more efficient engines, cleaner air, slower speeds, more time at home.

Home? Friends sometimes ask me pointedly, "Are you saying that a woman's place is in the home?" I reply, "Of course!" And then I add: "A man's place, too." Everybody's place is in the home. Work should always be the other place. I have never been opposed to anyone working hard, but it should always be with a clear sense of priorities. Nothing is worth the loss of a loving home. Where love is present, where parents put each other first, children look forward to coming home; they feel like counting the hours. We know what happens to young people who have no love to draw them home. Their parents' love is caught up in making money, accumulating possessions, getting ahead, enjoying themselves. With all this activity their lives may scarcely touch, let alone leave time for loving.

Material goals have served their purpose, but we now need a new set of inner goals even to enjoy material gains. How many people today live in loneliness, depression, selfishness, alienation, anger, fear? I don't think we need pride ourselves on having escaped the epidemic scourges of the Dark Ages if all we do is substitute plagues like these. I would like to hear someone today tell Meister Eckhart that he comes from the Dark Ages! He would retort, in the words of Saint Teresa: "Dark? I live in the light without a night." The rest of us, as the Gita puts it, are going about with our eyes closed in the middle of the night, calling the darkness day.

If you doubt this, look with some detachment at this morning's paper — any morning's paper. What do you think future generations will have to say about this twentieth century, this nuclear age of world wars? Certainly we have made great advances: in medicine, in genetics, in space travel, in communications, in any number of important fields. But where essentials are concerned, I don't think our civilization has made much progress at all.

In this next stage of civilization, it is the mystics we need to point the way. Mystics are great pioneers. Just one man like Saint Francis or Mahatma Gandhi, one woman like Saint Teresa, is enough to show the rest of us the goal to aim for, shining dimly through the haze of personal pursuits. In every age, the Bhagavad Gita promises, the Infinite comes to life in a finite personality to remind us what life is for. But we needn't wait for someone to come and lead us. The Infinite, the Lord of Love within your consciousness and mine, will inspire *us* — little people like you and me — to turn inward and learn to live as trustees for the rest of life. We need not wait for our own Gandhi. A number of mini-mahatmas will be enough to turn our times around.

Until we make this turning, however, our culture is drifting at sea. Only with a goal do momentary events become meaningful, for only then do we have a frame of reference into which events can fit. Our contemporary society does not believe in frames of reference; we have no real direction. Making money is not a goal, and accumulating possessions is little better. I doubt that there has been a time in history when wealth and possessions were within reach of so many; and I doubt there has been a time when the human being has been more lonely, more frustrated, more unsure of the future, more angry or violent or afraid, not only in this country but all over the world.

The mystics' answer is direct and down to earth: "Learn to discriminate between what is permanent and what is passing. Choose every day to do things that improve your health, promote lasting security, and deepen relationships—things that in the long run contribute to the well-being of your society and of the world. In this lies your happiness, your salvation, your very future."

"Our whole business in life," Augustine exhorts us, "is to restore to health the eye of the heart whereby God may be seen." Every one of us has the responsibility of evolution in his or her own hands. The Lord of Love is within us; the resources for spiritual evolution are our very own.

To fail to live up to this great challenge, my spiritual teacher used to say, is simply being irresponsible. This is not asking for perfection but merely expecting us to do our best to grow. If we do not do this much, we are depriving life of a contribution that only we can make. Spiritual living is responsible living. I am responsible not only for myself but for all of you, just as all of you are responsible for me.

This concern for the life and well-being of every creature, Saint Teresa says, is the beginning and end of the spiritual life:

> The contemplative life expands into activities which spring from this root and produce lovely and fragrant flowers. They spring from this tree of the love of God alone, for him alone, without anything of self-interest; and the fragrance of these flowers spreads all around, for the good of many. . . .

This is the ideal of discriminating action, which flows spontaneously from those who know the spiritual basis of life. It comes when we live in the highest state of awareness, when our lives become a benediction to every person and creature around us. We live then a truly selfless life, one in which we think never in terms of personal profit or pleasure but always in terms of global prosperity and world peace. For even these grand goals ultimately depend not on governments but on the selfless efforts of little people like you and me. In the long run, friendly persuasion is the only effective teacher. Human beings *are* educable; human beings can always grow. "If one man gains spiritually," Gandhi said, "the whole world gains with him."

A beautiful prayer from the ancient Hindu scriptures echoes in my heart always: "May all creatures be happy. May people everywhere live in abiding peace and love." For all of us are one, and joy can be found only in the joy of all.

May that prayer guide each of us in our daily lives.

PART 5

Instructions in Meditation

An Eight-Point Program

WHEN I CAME to this country on the Fulbright program in 1959, I was invited to speak to many groups of people on the source of India's ancient civilization. At the end of every talk a few thoughtful men and women would come up and ask me, "How can we bring these changeless values into our own daily life?"

"You don't have to change your religion," I assured them, "to do what I have done. The method of meditation I learned is universal. It can be practiced within the mainstream of any religious tradition, and outside all of them as well."

I began by teaching simply what I myself had been practicing for over a decade, illustrating from the scriptures and mystics of the world's great religions. Very quickly this became systematized into eight points, the first and most important of which is meditation. The next few pages are a short introduction to this eight-point program for spiritual growth, which is discussed fully in my books *Meditation* and *The Unstruck Bell*.

1. Meditation

The heart of this program is meditation: half an hour every morning, as early as is convenient. Do not increase this period; if you want to meditate more, have half an hour in the evening also, preferably at the very end of the day.

Set aside a room in your home to be used only for meditation and spiritual reading. After a while that room will become associated with meditation in your mind, so that simply entering it will have a calming effect. If you cannot spare a room, have a particular corner. Whichever you choose, keep your meditation place clean, well ventilated, and reasonably austere.

Sit in a straight-backed chair or on the floor and gently close your eyes. If you sit on the floor, you may need to support your back lightly against a wall. You should be comfortable enough to forget your body, but not so comfortable that you become drowsy.

Whatever position you choose, be sure to keep your head, neck, and spinal column erect in a straight line. As concentration deepens, the nervous system relaxes and you may begin to fall asleep. It is important to resist this tendency right from the beginning, by drawing yourself up and away from your back support until the wave of sleep has passed.

Once you have closed your eyes, begin to go *slowly,* in your mind, through one of the passages from the scriptures or the great mystics which I recommend for use in meditation. I usually suggest learning first the Prayer of Saint Francis of Assisi:

Lord, make me an instrument of thy peace.
Where there is hatred, let me sow love;
Where there is injury, pardon;
Where there is doubt, faith;
Where there is despair, hope;
Where there is darkness, light;
Where there is sadness, joy.

O divine Master, grant that I may not so much seek
To be consoled as to console,
To be understood as to understand,
To be loved as to love;
For it is in giving that we receive;
It is in pardoning that we are pardoned;
It is in dying to self that we are born to eternal life.

In memorizing the prayer, it may be helpful to remind yourself that you are not addressing some extraterrestrial being outside you. The kingdom of heaven is within us, and the Lord is enshrined in the depths of our own consciousness. In this prayer we are calling deep into ourselves, appealing to the spark of the divine that is our real nature.

While you are meditating, do not follow any association of ideas or try to think about the passage. If you are giving your attention to each word, the meaning cannot help sinking in. When distractions come, do not resist them, but give more attention to the words of the passage. If your mind strays from the passage entirely, bring it back gently to the beginning and start again.

When you reach the end of the passage, you may use it again as necessary to complete your period of meditation until you have memorized others. It is helpful to have a wide variety of passages for meditation, drawn from the world's major traditions. Each passage should be positive and practical, drawn from a major scripture or from a mystic of the highest stature. I especially recommend the following:

- the Twenty-third Psalm
- the Shema
- the Lord's Prayer
- the Beatitudes
- Saint Paul's "Epistle on Love" (1 Corinthians 13)
- Thomas a Kempis, *Imitation of Christ* III. 5 ("The Wonderful Effects of Divine Love")
- Chapters 1 and 26 of the Dhammapada of the Buddha
- Selections from the Bhagavad Gita:
  2.54 - 72 ("The Illumined Man")
  9.26 - 34 ("Make It an Offering")
  12.1 - 20 ("The Way of Love")
  18.49 - 73 ("Be Aware of Me Always")
- Ansari of Herat, "Invocations"

Most of these passages, along with many others equally

beautiful selected from the world's religions, can be found in my collection *God Makes the Rivers to Flow*.

The secret of meditation is simple: we become what we meditate on. When you use the Prayer of Saint Francis every day in meditation, you are driving the words deep into your consciousness. Eventually they become an integral part of your personality, which means they will find constant expression in what you do, what you say, and what you think.

2. Repetition of the Mantram

A mantram, or Holy Name, is a powerful spiritual formula which has the capacity to transform consciousness when it is repeated silently in the mind. There is nothing magical about this. It is simply a matter of practice, as you can verify for yourself.

Every religious tradition has a mantram, often more than one. For Christians, the name of Jesus itself is a powerful mantram. Catholics also use *Hail Mary* or *Ave Maria*. Jews may use *Barukh attah ʾAdonai*, "Blessed art thou, O Lord," or the Hasidic formula *Ribono shel olam*, "Lord of the universe." Muslims repeat the name of Allah or *Allahu akbar*, "God is great." Probably the oldest Buddhist mantram is *Om mani padme hum*, referring to the "jewel in the lotus of the heart." In Hinduism, among many choices, I recommend *Rama, Rama, Rama*, which was Mahatma Gandhi's mantram, or the longer mantram I received from my own spiritual teacher, my grandmother:

> *Haré Rama, Haré Rama,*
> *Rama Rama, Haré Haré,*
> *Haré Krishna, Haré Krishna,*
> *Krishna Krishna, Haré Haré.*

Select a mantram that appeals to you deeply. In many traditions it is customary to take the mantram used by your spiritual teacher. Then, once you have chosen, do not change your mantram. Otherwise you will be like a person digging shallow holes in many places; you will never go deep enough to find water.

Repeat your mantram silently whenever you get the chance: while walking, while waiting, while you are doing mechanical chores like washing dishes, and especially when you are falling asleep. You will find for yourself that this is not mindless repetition. The mantram will help to keep you relaxed and alert during the day, and when you can fall asleep in it, it will go on working for you throughout the night as well.

Whenever you are angry or afraid, nervous or worried or resentful, repeat the mantram until the agitation subsides. The mantram works to steady the mind, and all these emotions are power running against you which the mantram can harness and put to work.

3. Slowing Down

Hurry makes for tension, insecurity, inefficiency, and superficial living. I believe that it also makes for illness: among other things, "hurry sickness" is a major component of the Type A behavior pattern which research has linked to heart disease. To guard against hurrying through the day, start the day early and simplify your life so that you do not try to fill your time with more than you can do. When you find yourself beginning to speed up, repeat your mantram to help you slow down.

It is important here not to confuse slowness with sloth, which breeds carelessness, procrastination, and general inefficiency. In slowing down we should attend meticulously to details, giving our very best even to the smallest undertaking.

4. One-pointed Attention

Doing more than one thing at a time divides attention and fragments consciousness. When we read and eat at the same time, for example, part of our mind is on what we are reading and part on what we are eating; we are not getting the most from either activity. Similarly, when talking with someone, give him or her your full attention. These are little things, but all together they help to unify consciousness and deepen concentration.

Everything we do should be worthy of our full attention. When the mind is one-pointed it will be secure, free from tension, and capable of the concentration that is the mark of genius in any field.

5. Training the Senses

In the food we eat, the books and magazines we read, the movies we see, all of us are subject to the conditioning of rigid likes and dislikes. To free ourselves from this conditioning, we need to learn to change our likes and dislikes freely when it is in the best interests of those around us or ourselves. We should choose what we eat by what our body needs, for example, rather than by what the taste buds demand. Similarly, the mind eats too, through the senses. In this age of mass media, we need to be particularly discriminating in what we read and what we go to see for entertainment, for we become in part what our senses take in.

6. Putting Others First

Dwelling on ourselves builds a wall between ourselves and others. Those who keep thinking about *their* needs, *their* wants, *their* plans, *their* ideas cannot help becoming lonely and insecure. The simple but effective technique I recommend is to learn to put other people first — beginning within the circle of your family and friends, where there is already a basis of love on which to build. When husband and wife try to put each other first, for example, they are not only moving closer to each other. They are also removing the barriers of their ego-prison, which deepens their relationships with everyone else as well.

7. Reading in World Mysticism

We are so surrounded today by a low concept of what the human being is that it is essential to give ourselves a higher image. For this reason I recommend devoting half an hour or so each day to reading the scriptures and the writings of the great mystics of all religions. Just before bedtime, after evening meditation, is a particularly good time, because the thoughts you fall asleep in will be with you throughout the night.

There is a helpful distinction between works of inspiration and works of spiritual instruction. Inspiration may be drawn from every tradition or religion. Instructions in meditation and other spiritual disciplines, however, can differ from and even seem to contradict each other. For this reason, it is wise to confine instructional reading to the works of one teacher or path. Choose your teacher carefully. A good teacher lives what he or she teaches, and it is the student's responsibility to exercise sound judgment. Then, once you have chosen, give your teacher your full loyalty.

8. Spiritual Association

The Sanskrit word for this is *satsang,* "association with those who are spiritually oriented." When we are trying to change our life, we need the support of others with the same goal. If you have friends who are meditating along the lines suggested here, it is a great help to meditate together regularly. Share your times of entertainment too; relaxation is an important part of spiritual living.

ॐ

This eightfold program, if it is followed sincerely and systematically, begins to transform personality almost immediately, leading to profoundly beneficial changes which spread to those around us.